MW00427051

WHAT
GOD
IS
SAYING
TO YOU
TODAY

PETER
WALLACE

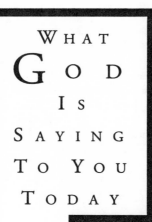

WHAT GOD IS SAYING TO YOU TODAY

PETER WALLACE

OLIVER NELSON

THOMAS NELSON PUBLISHERS
Nashville • Atlanta • London • Vancouver

Copyright © 1995 by Peter M. Wallace

All rights reserved. Written permission must be secured from the publisher to use or reproduce any part of this book, except for brief quotations in critical reviews or articles.

Published in Nashville, Tennessee, by Thomas Nelson, Inc., Publishers, and distributed in Canada by Word Communications, Ltd., Richmond, British Columbia.

Scripture texts are quoted from the *Contemporary English Version*. Copyright © by American Bible Society 1990, 1991, 1992, 1994.

Scripture quotations noted NKJV are from THE NEW KING JAMES VERSION. Copyright © 1979, 1980, 1982, 1990, Thomas Nelson, Inc., Publishers.

Library of Congress Cataloging-in-Publication Data

Wallace, Peter, 1954–
    What God is saying to you today / Peter Wallace.
        p.   cm.
    ISBN 0-8407-9204-2 (pbk.)
    1. Bible. O.T. Pentateuch—Meditations.   2. Bible. O.T. Historical Books—Meditations.   3. Devotional calendars. 4. Christian life—Meditations.   I. Title.
BS1205.4.W35   1995
242'.2—dc20   95-5198
                                                          CIP

Printed in the United States of America.

1 2 3 4 5 6—00 99 98 97 96 95

For my parents,
Aldred and Peggy Wallace,
my brothers, Greg and Vaughan,
and my sister, Ann

INTRODUCTION

There are any number of devotional books available today. My intention is that this book not be like any of them.

I hope you won't simply read this book; rather, use it as the basis of your meditations. Let it become for you a doorway into the presence of your heavenly Father, who welcomes you and delights in your spending time with Him. Let it be a springboard to launch your mind and catapult your heart into personal meditation and communion with the Lord.

What God Is Saying to You Today is one of a series of daily reading books designed to be flexible and interactive. The structure enables you to follow along as you feel most comfortable, and it encourages you to be open to the Spirit's leading in order to find the truth you need at the moment you read it.

There are at least three ways you can read this book.

1. *You can read it a page at a time, a day at a time.* Each page is dated and numbered. You can start out with Day 1 on January 1 (or whenever you like) and finish up with Day 366 (there's an extra

reading included for leap years). Of course, this is the traditional way of reading devotional books. And you may find it most convenient for you. But I would also urge you to consider one of a couple of alternative ways.

2. *Pray first, asking the Lord to direct your reading.* Then flip the book open to a page and read it. Or scan the verses to find one that hits you where you are. Now, you may be thinking this method sounds a bit strange. But give it a try, and sincerely ask for God's leading. You may find you need to read two pages or even three at one sitting to find the one that speaks loudest to you in your need at the moment.

3. A Subject Index is located in the back of the book to help you find a reading that focuses on a particular concept. So if you're feeling lonely or angry or fearful, or if you want some insight on worship or encouragement or faith, *look up these words and select a reading* that focuses on them. In this way your daily reading focuses on something relevant in your life at the moment.

You may think of yet another way to use the book. I hope you do because my goal is to encourage you to hear God's words as though for the first time. To hear them as though they were spoken directly to you. And to respond to them personally.

To this end, I encourage you to begin your time every day in prayer, to ask God to open your heart and mind to His insight and His will. Then read the page you've selected. It would be a good idea to keep a journal to record your thoughts and prayers. Let the reading launch your meditation on the words you read, particularly as they can be reflected in your life today. Then follow with a time of prayer, asking God to help you respond in whatever way He wills.

This isn't a devotional book; it's a workbook. The comments are designed to prod your heart and mind. I hope you will use this book to help you think and work through your struggles and frustrations in life. Let it be a guide to peace and serenity with your God.

If you benefit from using *What God Is Saying to You Today,* you may benefit from the companion volumes as well—*What Jesus Is Saying to You Today* and *What the Psalmist Is Saying to You Today.*

I would like to express my heartfelt appreciation to some special people in my life today who have contributed to my thinking and who challenge me to walk the path toward spiritual health and wholeness. They include my wife, Bonnie, my children Meredith and Matthew, my parents, Aldred and Peggy Wallace, my brothers Greg and Vaughan, my sister Ann Ballard, Gray Temple, Jr., Dr. Fred Hall, Harold McRae, Kathy Malcolm, Larry Smith, and my close friends Alan and Alex Charters, Cary McNeal, Kenneth King, Jon Franz, Jonathan Golden, David Hodge, Len Woods, Wesley Greer, Ben Sevison, John Lauber, Wayne Judge, Richard Beatty, Tim Toth, Craig Featherstone, Walt Wooden, Rick Dembicki, Mike Bailey, Dick Doster, and many other wise people with whom I work and live and play and worship. All are precious to me beyond words.

May God open your eyes through the reading of these words from the Old Testament historical books. And may my comments not get in His way or yours.

—Peter Wallace
Lawrenceville, Georgia

DAY 1

I command light to shine!

—Genesis 1:3

The first recorded words of the God of the universe form an invitation to you today. An invitation to see.

The first aspect of creation God spoke into being was the basic element upon which all life depends. Light gives life. Light fosters growth. Light reveals reality.

Scientists will argue and debate for centuries about the process of creation. And so will Christians. But we can know this: God created. The first thing He created was light. And the light still shines for you.

God's light enables you to see physically and spiritually. It can bathe you in nurturing warmth. It can uncover sin. It can show you the way to go. It can reveal all that God has created for your benefit.

God's Word is light. And in the process of reading it, praying through it, meditating on it, and working it out in your life, may you truly *see*.

JANUARY 1

DAY 2

I command the water under the sky to come together in one place, so there will be dry ground.
—Genesis 1:9

By the power of His word, God spoke the waters into existence, forming the seas, and the dry
land forming continents.

Still, the land and sea were devoid of any life.
On this second day of creation, God had simply
established the playing field. And what a playing
field it was!

The basics were in place for life to explode. All
life—in the seas, on land, in the air. But for one
brief period of time, all was quiet. Waiting.
Empty.

Life can feel like that. Your soul may feel devoid of life and energy. The rocks and dirt are
there, the basic elements in place, but nothing is
happening. Nothing is alive.

If that's how you feel today, this verse can give
you a new perspective. Life will come if you're
open to it. Like the empty earth yearning for innumerable life forms, yearn for God to fill you
up with life in all its fullness.

JANUARY 2

DAY 3

I command lights to appear in the sky and to separate day from night and to show the time for seasons, special days, and years. I command them to shine on the earth.

—Genesis 1:14–15

The Lord God established the heavenly lights—the sun and the moon—for two primary reasons: to give us a means to measure the passage of time, and to shed light on the earth.

It's clear that the sun sheds sufficient light to sustain life and enable us to see during the day, and the moon is a night light watching over us as we sleep. And yet they were also given to mark time, to help us regulate our lives.

Life is a cycle. Yet it is not a repetitive cycle. It is always new, always growing and changing, always moving forward.

Consider the assurance of the regular cycle of time. God offers us the comfort and guidance of the routine, yet promises us the newness and freshness of each new day. And we need both.

DAY 4

I command the ocean to be full of living creatures, and I command birds to fly above the earth. . . . I command the earth to give life to all kinds of tame animals, wild animals, and reptiles.

—Genesis 1:20, 24

God's seemingly infinite creativity populated the globe with life and energy. The earth came alive. The ecosystem was established. And God saw that it was good. Imagine His delight in the creation of so vast an array of living things.

God is infinitely creative. The more we learn about what He has done, the more our amazement grows.

He is still creative, even today. Even in your life. Bringing new experiences, new people, new places for your enjoyment, new lessons for living, new understanding and appreciation of yourself.

Applaud Him today for His creativity. Not only in the world, but in your life. Welcome it. Nurture it. Protect it. Stand in awe of it. And praise Him for it.

DAY 5

Now we will make humans, and they will be like us. We will let them rule the fish, the birds, and all other living creatures.

—Genesis 1:26

The image of God is found in every human being. God made us so.

In His wisdom, He endowed men and women with a free will to exercise their own choices within God-given limits. He imbued us with reason, self-consciousness, imagination, emotion, and creativity. He created our souls to be immortal.

And He gave us dominion over the living creatures of the earth. As He is our authoritative Ruler, so do we rule over the animal kingdom.

That isn't license to abuse or mistreat. Consider how God treats us—with compassion and dignity, with nurturing and care. That's how we're to exercise dominion over the animals. They were created to help meet our physical needs. But we were created to be like God in ruling over them.

How are you carrying out your reign?

JANUARY 5

Have a lot of children! Fill the earth with people and bring it under your control. Rule over the fish in the ocean, the birds in the sky, and every animal on the earth.

—Genesis 1:28

Our first parents were commanded by God to begin the family of humans, to fill the earth, and thereby to exercise dominion over all the created earth.

Clearly, man and woman were the crown of God's creativity, the climax of His handiwork. God gave them the world to enjoy and manage according to His will. Today, we're under the same orders.

There are far more of us today, however. The earth has been filled. The need is not to fruitfully multiply (although there is certainly no restriction on the size of our families). Rather, the charge remains to enjoy and manage the earth. To exercise dominion over it in terms of care and protection.

Whether you're married or single, a parent or not, you have been given the same responsibility that Adam and Eve accepted. Ask God how you can carry out that responsibility in His will today.

DAY 7

You may eat fruit from any tree in the garden, except the one that has the power to let you know the difference between right and wrong. If you eat any fruit from that tree, you will die before the day is over!

—*Genesis 2:16–17*

Why did God lay this restriction on Adam? Why hinder his free choice? It only set him up for a fall. And it was a very big fall.

Yet it was precisely Adam's free choice that was at stake in the Garden of Eden. God gave him free choice, and he—with Eve—chose to disobey.

All choices have consequences, good and bad. That is part of what makes the choice free.

But don't get sidetracked by this single restriction. Think of the choices that beckoned to Adam—and all of them free and open!

God's basic nature is giving. Yet, within guidelines and boundaries. Observe those limits, and you will never exhaust His supply. But test them, as Adam did, and expect consequences.

It is not good that man should be alone; I will make
him a helper comparable to him.

—*Genesis 2:18 (NKJV)*

Adam was alone, but he knew no other way.
Yet God knew it could be better.

So God created a "helper." Adam could not do
what he was supposed to do in life on his own.
He needed help.

And this helper was "comparable to him." Not
identical. Not opposite. But comparable.

What does that tell you about men and
women in general? How does that inform your
views? How does it affect your relationship with
your spouse? These are good questions and
worth meditating through with God.

It may not be easy to understand how it all
works out in life, but the bottom line is true: It
is not good to be alone.

You already know that. And today, there's
something you can do—with your spouse or a
friend—to deal with your aloneness.

DAY 9

Where are you?

—Genesis 3:9

Adam had sinned. He had willfully disobeyed God's command to refrain from eating the fruit of the tree of knowledge. Instantly, Adam's communion with God was broken.

"Where are you?" God asked. He reached out to the shattered man crouching in his humiliation, his nakedness, his sin.

God knew exactly where Adam was. He wasn't seeking information. He was inviting Adam to look at where he was, to see what had happened to him.

God had clearly established the terms of His relationship with Adam. Adam willfully broke those terms. God didn't leave Adam; Adam left God.

Yet God took the first step toward healing the breach. And the first step we must take in response is to recognize before God where we are and what we've done.

Take hope when you find yourself separated from God. His hands are extended to you in welcome. And He will take you from where you are to where you want to be.

JANUARY 9

Because of what you have done, you will be the only animal to suffer this curse—For as long as you live, you will crawl on your stomach and eat dirt. You and this woman will hate each other; your descendants and hers will always be enemies. One of hers will strike you on the head, and you will strike him on the heel.

—Genesis 3:14–15

In the form of a serpent, Satan sinned by encouraging Adam and Eve to sin. And Satan's sin was punished by God with a curse that would last through time.

In the curse, God cryptically revealed an event far distant in the future: the climax of human history when the Son of God and Satan would battle over the souls of humanity. Jesus Christ would be bruised and battered by the evil one; yet He would ultimately triumph over Satan in His resurrection over death.

Today, open your eyes. See Satan's attacks for what they are: a bald-faced attempt to keep you from experiencing the peace and joy that only God can give you.

You will suffer terribly when you give birth. But you will still desire your husband, and he will rule over you.

—Genesis 3:16

When was the last time you had a conflict with the opposite sex?

Odds are, one reason for the conflict is sourced in this consequence of Eve's sin. Because she willfully chose to disobey God's command by eating of the tree of knowledge, God was required by His holiness to deal with her sin.

Not only must women undergo intense pain in childbirth, but their relationships with men will often become power struggles. A woman will desire her husband, but he will be unable or unwilling to be or do what she desires. She will yearn to assume his leadership role, but he will rule over her. All this leads only to conflict, disagreement, misunderstanding, and more conflict.

Unless God enters the picture. Unless in a new arrangement, founded on Jesus Christ, the Spirit of God works through the individuals to provide patience, compassion, and love for each other.

The ground will be under a curse because of what you did. As long as you live, you will have to struggle to grow enough food. . . . You will have to sweat to earn a living; you were made out of soil, and you will once again turn into soil.

—Genesis 3:17, 19

Although Adam's community was agrarian, most of us aren't farmers today. But the principle still holds true. Life is hard. Work is harder. It's a constant frustration, a never-ending battle to support one's family, to make it all work.

What's the use? What's it all about? We work ourselves to exhaustion, and we ultimately die, returning to the dust from whence we came.

The truth is, it is useless. It is empty. And it is tough. But there is a different way. There is an opportunity to journey through life with a different set of priorities—empowered and supported by the One who created us.

Work will still be hard. Hassles will still dog us. But there will be hope and joy to carry us through it. And that's the only way to make life worth living.

DAY 13

These people now know the difference between right and wrong, just as we do. But they must not be allowed to eat fruit from the tree that lets them live forever.

—Genesis 3:22

Banished from Paradise. Adam had eaten of the tree of the knowledge of good and evil in direct disobedience of God's word. And before Adam could do any more damage, God removed him and Eve from the Garden of Eden.

The Bible never explains the tree of life. Nor had God ever prohibited eating its fruit. And yet, because Adam disobeyed and broke fellowship, it had become a danger to him.

Clearly, God was acting to protect Adam and Eve from greater danger to their souls. It opened up a life of challenge and growth, of depth and meaning, of achievement and power that perhaps would never have been possible within the Garden.

When God acts in our lives, it is always for our best. It may seem harsh, but it is an act of love and grace. Perhaps that's a reminder you need today.

What's wrong with you? Why do you have such an angry look on your face? If you had done the right thing, you would be smiling. But you did the wrong thing, and now sin is waiting to attack you like a lion. Sin wants to destroy you, but don't let it!

—*Genesis 4:6–7*

Cain was jealous and angry. He felt rejected and abandoned by God. His works weren't "good enough." And it drove him over the edge.

God pursued him, pushing him to confront his internal demons, to face the fact that his emotions were out of control. Cain rejected God's overtures to reconsider his motives, to pursue God in a healthy new way. He let sin enter the door of his life. And the results were devastating. With God's power, Cain could have ruled over the sin that gripped him. But he gave in to it.

If God is wooing you today as He did Cain, listen. Hear Him. And open yourself to His peace and strength.

DAY 15

Where is Abel?

—Genesis 4:9

Just as God pursued Adam after his sin—
"Where are you?"—so He pursues Cain after he
murdered his brother. But unlike Adam and Eve,
who admitted their sin, Cain lied. Cain had chosen his path, and in it lay falsehood and death.
"How should I know?" he answered. "Am I supposed to look after my brother?"

God didn't answer his question directly, but
the answer was clear: Yes.

If we are in a position to care for the well-
being of another human being, we are responsible to do whatever we can in our power. But
Cain had taken the opposite path. Rather than
deal with his internal problems with his brother,
he eliminated the supposed source of the problems.

God sets forth how He wants His children to
live. And in obedience, there are peace, joy, and
fulfillment. In disobedience, there can be only
estrangement and death.

Today, choose your path well. And when you
approach a brother or sister on the way, open
yourself to God in the interchange.

I won't let my life-giving breath remain in anyone forever. No one will live for more than one hundred twenty years.

—Genesis 6:3

God has limits. Sinful creatures that we are, we find it easier to focus on His forgiveness, His grace, His mercy. And He has those qualities in superabundance.

But in the days of Noah, humanity had reached a fever pitch of self-degradation, violence, and rebellion. Chaos reigned. And God had had enough of it. So He called on Noah to facilitate a new beginning.

It would do us well to focus on these seemingly opposite aspects of His nature: God's love and His wrath, His mercy and His judgment, His forgiveness and His holiness.

Rest assured, you are accepted in the blood of His Son, Jesus Christ. But know that God will always be working on you to smooth out the rough edges and bring you more fully into His will for you.

That may be painful at times. It may even feel like abandonment. But it's not. And knowing His unceasing love for you can help you conquer those feelings.

DAY 17

I'll destroy every living creature on earth! I'll wipe
out people, animals, birds, and reptiles. I'm sorry I
ever made them.

—Genesis 6:7

God's heart was broken. He looked on the face
of the earth and saw depravity and degradation,
violence and rebellion. And He was sorry. Even
so, judgment would come in the form of destruction.

Look on the holiness of God today. His purity
cannot be blemished. His righteousness cannot
tolerate willful disobedience. His mercy is tem-
pered with perfect justice. This same God rules
the world today. And He is actively working in
your life.

Surely, you've not pushed the limits as did the
human population of Noah's day. And in Christ,
you cannot exhaust His forgiveness and grace.

But realize how precious that forgiveness and
grace are. Don't allow yourself to take them for
granted.

Through Christ, God pours out an unlimited
flow of mercy toward us. Let that truth sink in
today. And thank Him for it.

But I solemnly promise that you, your wife, your
sons, and your daughters-in-law will be kept safe in
the boat.

—Genesis 6:18

In all the earth, covered over with sin and rebellion, God found a single righteous heart, a lone
soul who trusted Him. And God chose that man
to build the future of the human race upon.

God established a covenant with Noah—an
agreement to spare his life and the lives of his
family. But Noah had a gargantuan task to do to
protect them—and animal life—from the coming judgment: He had to build an ark. The whole
future of life on earth rested on his obedience.

In a world awash in chaos, God has established a covenant with you as well. It is an unbreakable bond between you and Him through
Jesus Christ.

He doesn't ask nearly as much of you. The future of life does not rest on your shoulders. He
simply asks that you enter into a living, growing
relationship with Him. That you go with Him
on the path toward wholeness. That you live
tuned in to His Spirit.

DAY 19

Bring out with you every living thing of all flesh that is with you: birds and cattle and every creeping thing that creeps on the earth, so that they may abound on the earth, and be fruitful and multiply on the earth.

—Genesis 8:17 (NKJV)

God's instructions to Noah give us a clue about His purpose for life.

Noah was to take along with him in the ark every living thing—birds, cattle, and every creeping thing—to replenish the earth after the Flood's destruction.

You see, God created life to be lived. To abound. To be fruitful. Read between the lines, and you see a life that's full of energy and zest and fun. Creatures that enjoy being alive and revel in their part of the earth's drama.

That's the kind of life God's children can have as well. He didn't make us to be bored or useless or empty. He made us to be active and abounding in joy, fulfillment, and purpose.

How does that ideal line up with your life today? It's possible only in the power of the Spirit of God.

Never again will I punish the earth for the sinful things its people do. All of them have evil thoughts from the time they are young, but I will never destroy everything that breathes, as I did this time.

—Genesis 8:21

Here's a promise God made to Himself. Even though He acknowledges the sinfulness of humanity—our hearts are sinful even from our youth—He will never take His anger out on the earth or on living creatures.

You can take some measure of comfort in that today.

You may be wrestling with desires you know are wrong or unhealthy. You may sometimes shock yourself with the depravity that springs out of nowhere in your mind. You may be beating yourself up for being such a sinful fraud.

Rest assured, you're not surprising God. He knows everything about you. And He still accepts you.

DAY 21

As long as the earth remains, there will be planting and harvest, cold and heat; winter and summer, day and night.

—Genesis 8:22

God's purpose for the earth has been revealed. Slowly, relentlessly, it unfolds in a rhythm that will never end—until the end of time. On and on it goes in a rhythm that provides stability and security and points to the One who set it all into motion, the One who even now consciously reigns over it moment by moment.

Life cycles in much the same way. You experience periods of planting truth and discovery about yourself, and then later you reap the benefits of that advance. You survive long, dark, cold periods of winter in your soul, and then the springtime comes and you bask in the warmth of acceptance and wholeness. You encounter a dark night of the soul, yearning for sleep, and then the dawn comes with fresh release.

Appreciate the rhythms of life. Draw strength from them. Honor the One who established them.

DAY 22

All animals, birds, reptiles, and fish will be afraid of
you. I have placed them under your control.

—Genesis 9:2

A new way of living began on earth after the
catastrophic flood.

God gave humanity animals to eat. They were
part of His provision for those who were to exercise dominion and stewardship over the reno-
vated planet. And because of humankind's
authority over them, the animals would fear us.

God has placed the care of the planet and its
inhabitants into the hands of humans. And we
are to exercise our dominion with care and concern for all living things and for the very stuff of
which the earth is made. All of it is given into our
hands. That can be an overwhelming responsibility—and one that's easily shirked.

Think about how this authority is exercised in
your life. How are you helping as a steward of the
earth?

I created humans to be like me, and I will punish
any animal or person that takes a human life. . . . If
a person takes the life of another, that person must
be put to death.

—Genesis 9:5–6

As the Creator of humans and the Giver of His
own image in them, God has ultimate authority
over the soul of every human.

Because of violence, murder, and all-around
chaos, civilization had deteriorated to the point
that God acted in judgment through the Flood.
Noah and his family would start over. But before
they did, God made clear the sanctity of human
life. Anytime a human being was slain—whether
by another human or by an animal—the mur-
derer was required to die. It's a paradox that a life
was required for taking a life, and yet it only un-
derscores the absolute gravity of the matter.

God created life, and it's up to Him to take it.
How sensitive are you to God's foundational appreciation for life? How would increased sensi-
tivity toward life change the way you live it?

DAY 24

I promise every living creature that the earth and those living on it will never again be destroyed by a flood.

—Genesis 9:11

As Noah began the task of repopulating the earth, God established His covenant, promising that never again would a flood destroy the earth.

The binding agreement was one-sided: God didn't ask anything from Noah at that point. He simply said we need not fear a globally destructive flood. It's unconditional, initiated by God, and everlasting. We can trust God to keep His word.

Perhaps you haven't been worrying much about being destroyed by a flood. But there may be other promises of God that you have lost sight of or doubted. Promises that He would never leave you or forsake you. That He would provide for your needs—physical, spiritual, and emotional—every day. That He would protect you from bearing more than you can take in life.

What promises are you doubting today? Review them with God in prayer. Trust His promises to you.

JANUARY 24

DAY 25

The rainbow that I have put in the sky will be my sign to you and to every living creature on earth. It will remind you that I will keep this promise forever.
—*Genesis 9:12–13*

Every time we see a rainbow, we gasp with delight, don't we? It's purely a natural phenomenon. And yet as believers, we know there's far more than that behind it.

Scholars believe the structure of the world before the Flood made rainbows impossible. It didn't rain; instead, vegetation was watered by springs within the earth. After the Flood, rains and storms could occur. And rainbows could span the skies.

God tells us every time we see a rainbow, we should remind ourselves of His unending love, His inexhaustible care, His perpetual peace.

There may be stormy rains in your life right now, but God's rainbow—His promise—is there, too. And it always will be.

DAY 26

These people are working together because they all speak the same language. This is just the beginning. Soon they will be able to do anything they want. Come on! Let's go down and confuse them by making them speak different languages—then they won't be able to understand each other.

—Genesis 11:6–7

W hy wouldn't God want all of us to be on the same wavelength, so we could live in harmony and unity together? Because it wouldn't happen. Odd as it may seem, God's act of confusing the languages of the people of earth was an act of gracious protection and care.

Left to its own devices, humanity will only get itself into trouble. In this case, the people decided together that the way to succeed was to build a tower to heaven. Then they could live as gods. So God graciously intervened.

The message of the story of the Tower of Babel is not that we shouldn't attempt to live in harmony and peace. It's that the only way to accomplish that is God's way, not ours.

Leave your country, your family, and your relatives
and go to the land that I will show you.

—Genesis 12:1

What would you do if God spoke to you and
told you to move away from your homeland,
your family, your friends, your present way of
life? Would you feel lost? Afraid? Unwilling to
yield control of your life? Be honest. It would be
a challenge, wouldn't it?

Especially if you—like Abram—had never
been away from home.

God told him to cut the ties. To say good-bye.
And to go to a land that He would show him.

Abram was a unique person, specially chosen
by God for a purpose. So the truth is, God probably won't be asking the same thing of you.

But He may ask you something else. Like giving up control of some of your money for an ur-
gent need in someone else's life. Or giving up a
dream that you know isn't in His will for you.
How willing are you to obey?

DAY 28

I will bless you and make your descendants into a great nation. You will become famous and be a blessing to others. I will bless anyone who blesses you, but I will put a curse on anyone who puts a curse on you. Everyone on earth will be blessed because of you.

—*Genesis 12:2–3*

Abram's obedience opened an almost overwhelming floodgate of God's promised blessing. It all happened, of course. And Abram's life still affects the world.

This is the kind of God that God is: One who desires more than anything to flood our lives with blessing and glory. One who desires to use us as a channel of blessing and encouragement to others. One who would do just that if we would only trust Him, open ourselves to Him, follow Him, obey Him, live in Him.

None of us will ever be an Abram. But we can be blessed of God. And we can in turn bless others.

So what is God saying to you today?

DAY 29

Look around to the north, south, east, and west.
—Genesis 13:14

God led Abram to a new land. Then God asked him to look around and see the blessing He was giving him. It stretched out before Abram in every direction. As far as he could see. And it was all for him.

Surely, it was more than Abram's mind could conceive, more than his heart could stand. His life would never be the same again.

Perhaps God has a blessing for you today. And all that you need to do is look around in every direction. See what's going on around you. See what waits for you just ahead. See where you are and where you want to be going. See a glimpse on the horizon of what God wants to surprise you with.

See the blessings all around—blessings you may have been blind to because you were so focused on the spot of ground where you stood.

Look around and see.

DAY 30

Now walk back and forth across the land, because I am giving it to you.

—Genesis 13:17

God showed Abram what He wanted to give to him. He invited Abram to claim it. To get up and walk through it—every square inch of it. Because it was his—God gave it to him.

Walk around, Abram. Bring your flocks and your companions with you. Settle in. This is home now. And it's all yours.

Abram obeyed. It wasn't enough to hear God's promise. It wasn't enough to stand there and stare at it. Abram had to walk through it. Accept it. Enter into it. Believe it. And live in it.

God has made numerous promises to you. You may have a sense where He wants to lead you personally.

Have you heard it? Have you seen it in your mind? Have you reached out for it and moved into it? It won't happen until you do.

Abram, don't be afraid! I will protect you and reward
you greatly.

—Genesis 15:1

Abram had been taken out of his simple way of
life in his own hometown and thrust into the ad-
venture of his life. He had just faced a pagan
king, who offered him gifts and worldly blessings. And he turned them down.

That can be an unsettling and very frightening
experience. But God spoke to Abram in reassuring tones.

In many ways, your life may parallel Abram's.
You've left the safety—or at least the familiar-
ity—of your family of origin. You've entered the
world. You battle daily with its enticements. And
it can be scary.

Hear God's words for you today. He will protect you. And knowing Him is the greatest, most
rewarding experience a human being can have on
this earth. Draw comfort and strength from that
truth today as you venture into the world.

Look at the sky and see if you can count the stars.
That's how many descendants you will have.

—Genesis 15:5

An old man, facing the end of his years. He had never held his own baby. Most other men would have sired a large family and been surrounded by children, grandchildren, and even great-grandchildren by that time in their lives. But not Abram. Yet God was promising him not only an heir but a sky full of descendants.

In but a few hundred years, God will have kept this promise. And today, the number of physical and spiritual descendants would be impossible to enumerate.

Imagine hearing God's words and staring up into the starry darkness. Would you have had the faith to comprehend it? The trust to believe it? The acceptance to rest in it?

God is setting something before you—a promise about your work, your relationships, your ministry, your future. Do you hear Him? Do you trust Him? Look into the starry night sky, and believe.

DAY 33

I brought you here from Ur in Chaldea, and I gave you this land.

—*Genesis 15:7*

Abram was a nobody. A citizen of Ur. A simple man. The power of God intersected with his uncomplicated life and, through it, changed the world. It all started when the Lord called him out of his homeland, took him to a new land, and gave it to him.

The Bible is full of stories of simple, ordinary people through whom God wrought miracles and changed the course of history. They may have been simple and ordinary, but they were all marked by one thing: unquestioning obedience. When God spoke, they heard Him. They believed Him. They accepted what God gave them to be and to do.

Not that they didn't experience doubts. Not that they didn't argue and even wrestle with God. But that was part of the process of their obedience.

The Word of God can speak to you today. And the power of God can work through you today. But only if your heart is open and ready for it.

FEBRUARY 2

Abram, you will live to an old age and die in peace. But I solemnly promise that your descendants will live as foreigners in a land that doesn't belong to them. They will be forced into slavery and abused for four hundred years. But I will terribly punish the nation that enslaves them, and they will leave with many possessions.

—Genesis 15:13–15

Sometimes we think we'd like to know exactly what the future holds for us. Of course, with the good news there will be bad—life is like that. In Abram's case, God made it clear what would happen.

Most of us are never given the opportunity to know the future. The truth is, we would probably be overwhelmed by it.

Instead, God has given us each moment to live in, moment after moment. He calls us to trust Him for each day, day by day. And He gives us everything we need to make it through each day. Thank Him for that today.

I am God All-Powerful. If you obey me and always do right, I will keep my solemn promise to you and give you more descendants than can be counted.

—Genesis 17:1–2

God called Abram to obey Him, to live in such a way as to reflect God's values and purposes. And when Abram obeyed God, He would act as El Shaddai, God All-Powerful.

That's the way His covenant was established with Abram. And is established with you.

It's not that He expects perfection from us. Rather, He wants us to obey Him, to build our lives on the foundation of following Him.

We'll make mistakes along the way. Our hearts will rebel from time to time. Still, His relationship with us will be strong. He will always be the all-powerful One for us. Ask Him for the strength you need to stay with Him today.

DAY 36

I promise that you will be the father of many nations. That's why I now change your name from
Abram to Abraham.

—Genesis 17:4–5

The name *Abram* in Hebrew means "exalted father." God added to it, giving the man He had
chosen a new name: *Abraham,* or "exalted father
of many."

By giving him a new name, God set Abraham
apart. He demonstrated His authority over Abraham. And He made clear His commitment to
keep His promise to Abraham regarding his descendants.

Think about your name. Do you know what
it means? (Look it up in a baby name book soon
if you don't.) What do you like about your name?
What would you change? How has its meaning
been true in your life? In what ways would you
like to see your life reflect the meaning of your
name more closely?

Talk to God today about your name and how
you'd like to live in light of its meaning. What do
you think God would call you?

DAY 37

I will give you and them the land in which you are
now a foreigner. I will give the whole land of Canaan
to your family forever, and I will be their God.

—*Genesis 17:8*

God's promise to Abraham included blessing
not only to him but also to his descendants. And
the ultimate picture was a nation bursting at the
seams in the glorious land of Canaan. And God
ruling over them all.

But the reality of the moment was something
else entirely. Abraham was virtually alone in a
strange land. Sure, the land may have been his by
divine right, but tell that to the current inhabitants—whom Abraham didn't even know.

It didn't look good. Surely, the only thing that
got him through the early lean times was the lav-
ish promise God held out for him. But that was
enough.

Your present reality may look pretty lonely
and bleak as well. It won't stay that way. You will
grow, become more comfortable, expand your
network, build strong relationships, and see the
promise of your life fulfilled unfolding before
your very eyes. Take comfort in that hope. You
may need it today.

FEBRUARY 6

DAY 38

Why did Sarah laugh? Does she doubt that she can have a child in her old age? I am the LORD! There is nothing too difficult for me. I'll come back next year at the time I promised, and Sarah will already have a son.

—Genesis 18:13–14

When Sarah heard about God's promise of an heir, she did what just about any woman of her advanced age would do: laugh in disbelief. She was old. How could it possibly happen?

God called her on it, asking Abraham why she would react in such a way. Because nothing is too difficult for the Lord.

What promise of God are you having trouble believing today? What causes you to laugh in disbelief or weep in despair of believing? It's time to laugh in joy rather than in doubt.

DAY 39

I have chosen him to teach his family to obey me forever and to do what is right and fair. Then I will give Abraham many descendants, just as I promised.
—*Genesis 18:19*

God made Himself known to Abraham not just for Abraham's sake.

Yes, Abraham lived obediently and enjoyed God's blessing. But God charged Abraham to pass the blessing on to his family members, teaching them the ways of God, living before them as an example. Because only by following in father Abraham's footsteps would his descendants fulfill the promise of God for a great and holy nation.

God deeply desires that you pass on what you know about Him to the next generation. To live righteously and healthfully in their presence. To let the light of His love shine through you to touch them.

How conscious are you of the importance of this role in your life? Acknowledge God in everything you do, and let Him work through you for everyone's good.

FEBRUARY 8

DAY 40

Go get Isaac, your only son, the one you dearly love! Take him to the land of Moriah, and I will show you a mountain where you must sacrifice him to me on the fires of an altar.

—Genesis 22:2

Wait a minute! Abraham had waited all his life for his son. God had miraculously promised the boy's birth, then delivered on His promise. But He wanted Abraham to sacrifice Isaac? How could that be?

What would you think of a God like that? Would you obey?

Abraham did. The Bible merely says the next morning, Abraham got up, got his donkey ready for the trip to Mount Moriah, and took Isaac with him.

He didn't question. He didn't doubt. He simply obeyed and trusted God for the outcome. His faith in God was strong.

What an example of unquestioning obedience! How strong would you be in a situation like that? How strong would you like to be? Perhaps today God will give you a test, too.

Don't hurt the boy or harm him in any
way! . . . Now I know that you truly obey God, because you were willing to offer him your only son.
—Genesis 22:12

It was the ultimate test: Was Abraham willing to
put to death the most important thing in his life?
Would he sacrifice the human being who meant
the world to him, just because God asked him
to?

Yes. And at the last moment, the obedient
Abraham heard God call out to him to stop.
Abraham's actions revealed that in truth, the
most important thing in his life was his relationship with God, not with his son.

And that may be what God is asking you to
consider today. What are your priorities? What
are the loves of your life? What gives you joy and
hope and pleasure? What do you worship?

Those things may not be wrong in themselves.
But God may be asking you to sacrifice them, to
reveal to you the priorities you're really living by.
Would you be willing to obey today?

DAY 42

You were willing to offer the LORD your only son, and so he makes you this solemn promise, "I will bless you and give you such a large family, that someday your descendants will be more numerous than the stars in the sky or the grains of sand along the beach. . . . You have obeyed me, and so you and your descendants will be a blessing to all nations on earth."

—Genesis 22:16–18

Abraham was certainly overwhelmed with both fear and relief. On the side of Mount Moriah, he had prepared to kill his own son—until God stopped him.

In response to that unquestioning obedience, God reiterated His eternal blessing on Abraham and his descendants.

It's a tidal wave of blessing, so big it can't be imagined. It's as big as the heavens and the earth. And its impact will reverberate through human experience forever.

Open yourself to God's word for you today. Prepare yourself to obey. Then stand back and watch God bless you in amazing ways.

You will live there as a foreigner, but I will be with you and bless you. I will keep my promise to your father Abraham by giving this land to you and your descendants.

—Genesis 26:3

The promise God made to Abraham passed to the next generation: God instructed Isaac to dwell in the land that would belong to him and all his descendants.

We, too, are to live within the scope that God has ordained for us, in the "land" He has given us.

When we journey through life trusting God to lead us, be with us, and bless us, we can be free to take it as it comes. We can know that God is working, that life is giving us everything we need, that our circumstances are here for a reason.

We can trust God. And that security can banish fear and weariness, confusion and frustration. The alternative is to wander aimlessly, constantly seeking more and more—of what, we're not quite sure.

DAY 44

Don't be afraid! I am the God who was worshiped by your father Abraham, my servant. I will be with you and bless you, and because of Abraham I will give you many descendants.

—Genesis 26:24

God adopted Isaac as His own, just as He had Isaac's father. And He passed the blessing and the promise on to him.

In some ways, that blessing continues to be shared, one by one, as we come to the Lord in faith. In salvation through Christ, we are adopted as God's own. To us, also, He sends His comforting promise.

Once we were lost and alone in this world; now the God of the universe dwells with us and walks with us. Once we were subject to fear and emptiness; now we can experience an abundance of peace, joy, and contentment with God.

Once we faced a bleak and dark future; now we can anticipate glory, light, and perfect bliss in eternity.

Are you experiencing the blessings of God's adoption of you today? It's all there for you, ready to be taken, experienced, enjoyed. Today.

Your name will no longer be Jacob. You have wrestled with God and with men, and you have won. That's why your name will be Israel.

—Genesis 32:28

The night before Jacob's encounter with his brother Esau, a man came to Jacob and wrestled with him all night. Jacob put up a valiant struggle until the stranger touched his hip and caused a permanent injury.

Jacob's revealing his name to the stranger was a form of surrender. But the stranger renamed him Israel, which means "Wrestler with God" and "Prince with God." Both were true. And Jacob, now Israel, realized he had been wrestling with God Himself.

Perhaps you can identify with Jacob. Running scared, facing an event that overwhelms you, desperate for God's salvation. The struggle seems like a physical wrestling match—until you come to the end of yourself and can trust only God. The results of such struggle are always positive. Our souls are healthier, our hearts are stronger, our spirits are freer.

DAY 46

Return to Bethel, where I appeared to you when you were running from your brother Esau. Make your home there and build an altar for me.

—Genesis 35:1

Jacob was in big trouble once again. He faced a very angry enemy nation. God spoke to him, advising him to go to Bethel and dwell there. There, Jacob consecrated his entire family to the Lord, bathing them in His protection and care.

There's a lesson here for us. When we face a threatening circumstance, our first response should be to listen to God. The lesson is not that we should always remove ourselves from such circumstances; other times God had His people stay and fight, to face the battle in His power. The lesson is to be sensitive to God's will in any particular situation. And then to obey it.

As you face a seeming crisis today, pray. God wants your best in it.

DAY 47

I am God All-Powerful. . . . You will have many
children. Your descendants will become nations, and
some of the men in your family will even be kings. I
will give you the land that I promised Abraham and
Isaac, and it will belong to your family forever.

—Genesis 35:11–12

In response to Jacob's consecration of his family,
God restated His promise—originally made to
Abraham, then to Isaac, and now to Jacob. The
promise was his. And so was the responsibility of
dwelling in the land, filling it, and living under
God's care.

From generation to generation the promise
was passed. And now, in a sense, it is in your
hands. God has given you a life to live. It is your
land. He is the ultimate ruler; you are the steward. He will never leave you. But He deeply desires that you live under His authority and care.

Your life is like the land Jacob inherited.
Awash with threats as well as opportunities.
Filled with hard work as well as freedom. And
God is there.

FEBRUARY 16

DAY 48

I am God, the same God your father worshiped. Don't be afraid to go to Egypt. I will give you so many descendants that one day they will become a nation. I will go with you to Egypt, and later I will bring your descendants back here. Your son Joseph will be at your side when you die.

—Genesis 46:3–4

A word of reassurance and comfort came to Jacob from God. And once again He painted the future in broad strokes. All is well, and all will be well. That is His message.

There will be good times and bad Life and death. Growth and frustration. Freedom and slavery. But God will be there through it all.

That's His message for you today. Life will never be a bed of roses. There are some sand dunes to encounter in the desert. But He will go through it with you. Teaching you, guiding you, releasing you, using you, comforting you. Draw comfort and strength from that promise today as you walk with Him.

DAY 49

Don't come any closer. Take off your sandals—the ground where you are standing is holy.

—Exodus 3:5

Moses was minding his own business, watching his flock of sheep, when he encountered a bush that burned without being consumed. And the Lord spoke to him there on a rocky mountain that suddenly became holy ground.

Moses' sandals had walked through the dirt of human existence. They represented the wayward steps of humanity apart from God. And in His holiness, God could not tolerate them.

Not that He doesn't accept our human frailties and needs, or that He is unable to reach to us in our depths of sin. But this is a reminder of His absolute purity and holiness, which can cleanse us and free us from the sludge we bring with us into His presence.

Come into His presence today. Take off your shoes. Release your needs. He will take them and cleanse them. He will free you from their pain. Perhaps just for a moment. Perhaps forever. Where you are right now is holy ground. Because God is with you.

DAY 50

I am the God who was worshiped by your ancestors Abraham, Isaac, and Jacob.

—*Exodus 3:6*

In the presence of God on the mountain Moses heard the voice of God from the burning bush. God traced His lineage, so to speak, from Moses to his father, back to Abraham, Isaac, and Jacob.

And in response, "Moses was afraid to look at God, and so he hid his face" (v. 6). In the light of God's holy fire, Moses was ashamed. His sinfulness covered him. He couldn't look at the absolute purity before him, or he would have been destroyed. Later, on Mount Sinai, Moses would meet God virtually face-to-face and ask to see His glory.

Things change. Our perceptions of ourselves and of God grow and mature. Progress is made; maturity is reached; healthiness and wholeness are achieved.

Reaching those goals requires time. Understanding. And the grace of God. God would delight to give that in abundance to you.

I have surely seen the oppression of My people who are in Egypt, and have heard their cry because of their taskmasters, for I know their sorrows.

—Exodus 3:7 (NKJV)

Overwhelmed by God's holiness, Moses heard comforting truths that must have reverberated in the core of his soul.

"I have surely seen the oppression of My people." *God sees us.* He watches us as a loving Father watches His playful children, struggling to walk, working hard to learn how to live, making mistakes, falling down, running around in fear, giving in to sin, taking small steps of growth.

"I have heard their cry because of their taskmasters." *God hears us.* He hears our wails of grief, our cries for help, our shouts of victory. He hears our prayers in good times and bad. And He doesn't just listen, He hears.

"I know their sorrows." *God knows us.* Inside and out. We can rest in the knowledge that He hasn't forgotten us or turned His back on us. That is not His nature.

I have come down to rescue them from the Egyptians. I will bring my people out of Egypt into a country where there is good land, rich with milk and honey.

—Exodus 3:8

God answered the cries of His people for help. He provided all that was needed. He promised an even brighter future.

The Israelites suffered under the oppression of the Egyptians for hundreds of years. It was time for deliverance from the prison of slavery to the paradise of their own homeland. And what a land it would be, "a good land, rich with milk and honey."

Today, God is assuring you that He knows your needs. He knows where you need to go from here. He knows the job you need, the home you need, the relationships you need, the answers you need.

And He has a plan to deliver you from where you are to where you ought to be. You may not get all the details today. But you can rest in the knowledge that His plan will come to pass.

I will be with you. And you will know that I am the one who sent you, when you worship me on this mountain after you have led my people out of Egypt.

—Exodus 3:12

It was a bombshell in Moses' soul. The God of Abraham, Isaac, and Jacob, the Lord of the universe, had chosen him to lead the people of Israel to freedom.

Moses' response is certainly easy to identify with: "Who am I to go to the king and lead your people out of Egypt?" (v. 11). Or, in the vernacular, "Who—me?"

There was no way Moses felt he had the resources to accomplish what God was giving him to do. How could it be? So God answered him, "I will be with you."

You may face a task that seems just as overwhelming to you. "I will be with you," God says to you. To give you power, guidance, and strength, in the proper timing, in the most effective way.

I am the eternal God. So tell them that the LORD, whose name is "I Am," has sent you.

—*Exodus 3:14*

The nation of Israel had languished in slavery for more than four hundred years, away from their homeland. Moses questioned whether the people would even listen to him, for many of the people had forgotten who their God was.

So he asked God, "But what should I say, if they ask me your name?" (v. 13).

And God answered that His name is "I Am." It's the only time God ever explained His Hebrew name, YHWH (often spelled Yahweh or Jehovah). The name is a form of the verb "to be."

God is the One who is. The One who is ever present. The One who has always existed and will always exist. He was present with the Israelites. He is still present with His children. Always ready to hear. Always able to help.

So I will use my mighty power to perform all kinds of miracles and strike down the Egyptians. Then the king will send you away.

—Exodus 3:20

God made it sound so easy. He told Moses how He would gain freedom for the nation of Israel from their Egyptian bondage. It was just a matter of using His power, performing some miracles, and then Pharaoh would let them go.

You know it's a true description, but there was much more to it. A series of devastating plagues. A hardened heart. An angel of death. A terrifying escape. A relentless pursuit. A dramatic crossing of the sea—and that was just the beginning.

God knew exactly what lay ahead for the Israelites in every detail. But He chose to reveal certain amounts in small doses.

In the same way, God will tell you everything you need to know right now. No more, no less. You have everything you need to make wise decisions and healthy choices as you walk the path toward wholeness.

Who makes people able to speak or makes them deaf or unable to speak? Who gives them sight or makes them blind? Don't you know that I am the one who does these things?

—*Exodus 4:11*

Moses tried just about every excuse to duck the call of God. Then he argued, "I have never been a good speaker. I wasn't one before you spoke to me, and I'm not one now. I am slow at speaking, and I can never think of what to say" (v. 10).

But that didn't cut it with God. He created the very mouth of man. So He can empower that mouth and use it for His own purposes.

God is sovereign. So when He calls us to do something, He will empower us to fulfill it. If we are to speak, He will give us the words. If we are to serve, He will give us the strength. Whatever He gives us to do, He will help us do it.

Now go! When you speak, I will be with you and give you the words to say.

—Exodus 4:12

A task looms before us. We're fearful of it. Convinced of our impending failure. Devoid of any strength or assurance of success. And God tells us to go. To go regardless. And if we take that first step, we will discover His abundant provision to fulfill His calling.

In Moses' case, God promised to be with him, to tell him what to say to the people and to Pharaoh.

In your case, He will give you everything you need to succeed. Fear may be keeping you from that first step. Take a risk. Take the first step. Go. And find out firsthand how God can provide whatever you need to fulfill His call on your life.

My name is the LORD. But when I appeared to Abraham, Isaac, and Jacob, I came as God All-Powerful and did not use my name.

—Exodus 6:2–3

As Moses undertook the task God set before him, God graciously reminded him who He is and how He will provide.

A reminder that He is the Lord—YHWH. The One who is always present, always existing, always here with us.

A reminder that He is the God of Abraham, Isaac, and Jacob. He has proven Himself time and again with His people. And He will do so again.

A reminder that He is God All-Powerful.

And He is the God Moses knew better than Abraham, Isaac, and Jacob ever did.

Guess what: You can know Him even better than Moses. You have the complete revelation, the Bible, to guide you to Him. You have the living Lord, Jesus Christ, as your Savior. You have the power of the Holy Spirit dwelling within you.

I made an agreement and promised them the land of Canaan, where they were living as foreigners. Now I have seen how the people of Israel are suffering because of the Egyptians, and I will keep my promise.
—*Exodus 6:4–5*

A lot of believers keep their emotions bottled up. They don't want to bother God with their problems. They can handle the situation themselves. The truth is, they can't. And keeping all those feelings and thoughts bottled up only builds to a level of spontaneous combustion.

Look at the Israelites. They were suffering and "groaning" (6:5 NKJV). God heard them and promised to deliver them. When they wept, they really wept. When they celebrated, they danced all night. And God was present in the release of those emotions.

You may need help to express your feelings in a healthy, helpful way. If so, find a friend, a counselor, or a pastor to talk to. Today.

Here is my message for Israel: "I am the LORD! And with my mighty power I will punish the Egyptians and free you from slavery."

—Exodus 6:6

God promised to free the children of Israel. They were under the terrible burden of slavery in Egypt. And they had been for more than four hundred years. But God would bring them out from under those circumstances.

They were in bondage—not only in the grueling work of slavery, but unable even to live in their own land. They were in a precarious situation, living under a hothead Pharaoh, surrounded by a mighty army and a deadly desert. They'd had no leadership in centuries.

But God would free them—powerfully, amazingly, certainly.

What in your life feels like slavery to you right now? An addictive habit? A bad relationship? Emotional pain from the past?

God is prepared to free you, too.

DAY 61

I will accept you as my people, and I will be your God. Then you will know that I was the one who rescued you from the Egyptians.

—Exodus 6:7

In effect, God was adopting the Israelites as His very own. With all the rights and privileges that entailed.

The Israelites were certainly nothing special. They were just one of a number of Middle Eastern tribal assemblages. But God chose them and set them apart. They became His instrument to the world they lived in. They became His children.

He has done the same for us. He has taken us as His own. He has become our Father. And we can know—just as the Israelites did—that He is the God who acts, teaches, works, loves, accepts, strengthens, and comforts us throughout our own journey out of the desert.

Talk to your heavenly Father today about your relationship: where it has been, where it is, where you want it to be. He yearns to hear from you.

MARCH 1

Each family must take care of its animal until the evening of the fourteenth day of the month, when the animals are to be killed. Some of the blood must be put on the two doorposts and above the door of each house where the animals are to be eaten.

—Exodus 12:6–7

God communicated His plan for the release of the Israelites from Egypt. It involved sacrificing unblemished lambs and spreading the blood around the doorways.

The concept of animal sacrifice may make us feel uncomfortable today. But any relationship with God is based on the shedding of blood.

One single sacrifice, one instance of shed blood, has provided the way for believers today to approach God in His holiness. That was through the death of His Son, Jesus Christ, on the cross. In Him we no longer need to observe the complicated system of animal sacrifice. He has opened the way for us to God forever. Walk in that way today.

That same night I will pass through Egypt and kill the first-born son in every family and the first-born male of all animals. I am the LORD, and I will punish the gods of Egypt.

—Exodus 12:12

The night of judgment was coming. God was preparing to go to work. He would rescue His people. He would protect them from the judgment of death. He would judge the godless Egyptians in a way they would never forget.

Judgment is never a pretty sight. And it's a side of God that we may have trouble understanding or accepting. We prefer to think of God in His glory, love, mercy, and grace.

But God's holiness and perfection are unrelenting. In His perfect timing, He must judge evil and give it the punishment it deserves.

You need not fear it, though. Remember that in the Passover, God's action was taken totally on behalf of His children, whom He loved and provided for in every way. You will never experience the wrath of God. That has been spent already on your behalf.

DAY 64

Stay away from yeast, no matter where you live. No one is allowed to eat anything made with yeast!

—Exodus 12:20

Just before the Israelites' release from Egypt, God called His people to observe the Feast of Unleavened Bread, which follows Passover. Why unleavened bread? They were preparing to leave in a hurry—hundreds of thousands of people streaming from the city toward freedom. If they had to wait around for the bread to rise, they wouldn't have been ready to go at a moment's notice. Made without yeast, the bread was flat and crackery, so it wouldn't spoil on their journey.

Leavened bread symbolized unbelief, unreadiness, and lack of confidence in God's promise of freedom. Because of that, yeast came to symbolize the moral decay that bloats humanity.

Is there leaven in your life hindering your obedience to God? Ask God to help you discern it. And remove it.

MARCH 4

DAY 65

Dedicate to me the first-born son of every family and the first-born males of your flocks and herds. These belong to me.

—Exodus 13:2

In Egypt, the Lord's "angel that brings death" (12:23) took the firstborn of every family and flock. The blood of the lamb spared the Israelites the same fate.

But God instructed His people to sanctify—or set apart—to Him all the firstborn of Israel, both people and animals. They were His to do with as He willed. They belonged to Him. And the concept of giving the first to God would saturate the thinking of the Israelites.

Unfortunately, we often lose sight of that priority. We tend to think that everything we own is actually ours. Including our children.

The truth is, God owns everything. Our income, our possessions, our property, our families—it's all in His hands. He has given it into our care to protect it, use it, invest it, and share it.

If He took everything away from you, would you still have enough? Yes.

MARCH 5

Why do you keep calling out to me for help? Tell the Israelites to move forward. Then hold your walking stick over the sea. The water will open up and make a road where they can walk through on dry ground.

—Exodus 14:15–16

God had miraculously freed them from Egypt, gotten them out of the city, judged the enemy decisively, and then led them to the edge of the Red Sea. And Pharaoh's army was hot on their trail. Immediately, all faith evaporated. "It would have been better for us to serve the Egyptians than to die in the wilderness," they cried.

Moses assured them of God's protection and care. Then God spoke: Why do you doubt that I will take care of you? Why are you afraid?

God told them to move forward. And He saw to it that the way opened up. It was there all the time. All it took was faith to take the next step forward.

Perhaps you're crying to God for help. You can rely on Him to open up the way. Just take the first step forward.

DAY 67

I will send bread down from heaven like rain. Each day the people can go out and gather only enough for that day. That's how I will see if they obey me.

—Exodus 16:4

God would drop bread—manna—from heaven on the land. All the people had to do was go out and gather a certain amount per person. That was all there was, day by day. Everything they'd need, no more and no less.

Trying to gather more than they needed to save for tomorrow would show their lack of faith. They would fail the test.

God gives us everything we need for each day. That's true physically, spiritually, and emotionally. It may not land right on our plates. We may have to go out and gather it. But it's there, waiting for us. And it's exactly what we need.

If you're feeling needy today, ask yourself how much you really need what you think you need. If it's genuine, then go out and gather. And enjoy the manna God gives you.

MARCH 7

I have heard my people complain. Now tell them that each evening they will have meat and each morning they will have more than enough bread. Then they will know that I am the LORD their God.

—Exodus 16:12

As the Israelites wandered in the desert, again they started complaining: "We're going to starve to death out here in the wilderness!"

So the Lord promised to provide meat for the evening and bread for the morning. And He fulfilled that promise.

Once again they had ample opportunity to realize that God was who He said He was. He possessed all power and authority over nature and humanity. He was able to meet every need.

Consider your complaints today. Recognize them for what they may be. If they're not genuine needs, perhaps they're little indicators of doubt and fear. If so, give them to God. And wait in faith for your meat or manna.

Tomorrow is the Sabbath, a sacred day of rest in honor of me. So gather all you want to bake or boil, and make sure you save enough for tomorrow.

—*Exodus 16:23*

The Sabbath was (and is) important to God. So important that He provided enough provisions to last for two days once every week.

He commanded His people to take care of all their need to work before the seventh day. He intended that special day to be a time of rest, recuperation, and renewal. It would be a time His people could focus on Him while gaining fresh resources for a new week—physically, spiritually, and emotionally.

Unfortunately, the concept of the Sabbath is virtually lost in our society. Examine your calendar today. Reconsider your schedule. Are you taking time off to rest your heart, mind, soul, and body?

It's important to God. It should be important to you.

When you get to the rock at Mount Sinai, I will be there with you. Strike the rock with the stick, and water will pour out for the people to drink.

—Exodus 17:6

Complain, complain, complain. If there was one thing the Israelites did magnificently, it was complaining. They had run out of water. They were in the desert. But rather than ask God to help, they complained to Moses.

At least Moses had the presence of mind to run to God and ask for water. And as soon as he did, God told him how to get it.

How often do we shortchange ourselves by failing to ask God for what we need? How often have we turned a need over to God, then quickly taken it back to worry about it some more? Sometimes we look a lot more like the Israelites than like Moses.

If you're thirsty today, make your needs a matter of fervent prayer. God will answer.

Write an account of this victory and read it to Joshua. I want the Amalekites to be forgotten forever.

—Exodus 17:14

The Amalekites were a violent, deceitful, obstreperous people who took it upon themselves to be a troublesome enemy to the Israelites. They attacked the nation, and Joshua was called up to fight back. God sent His power through Moses' upstretched arms as they fought, and the victory was sure.

Then God encouraged Moses to write an account of what happened, to remember what God had done through His people. He also made a promise to eventually remove every trace of the Amalekites from the face of the earth. And He suggested recounting the event to Joshua, who in days ahead would need the encouragement.

Do you record the victories of your life, big and small? In times of discouragement and disappointment, you too can review your victories and rebuild your hope, restore your strength, and renew your spirit.

Now therefore, if you will indeed obey My voice and keep My covenant, then you shall be a special treasure to Me above all people; for all the earth is Mine.

—Exodus 19:5 (NKJV)

The nation of Israel had been called to be God's people, to obey Him, to keep the relationship with Him pure and strong. And in so doing, they were uniquely blessed.

God owns everything on the earth. Every human soul belongs to Him. Even the darkest, foulest, emptiest life is ultimately in His hands.

But those who are called to follow Him are a "special treasure" to Him. And you are part of that treasure.

Think about that today. He holds you in a special place. He treasures you. He delights in watching you grow. He shines on you with His warm love and care.

In all the universe, you exist in a unique place. And yet you are surrounded by a vast company of kindred spirits. Draw comfort from your relationship with God and your companionship with fellow believers. That is the only source of strength that lasts.

You will be my holy nation and serve me as priests.

—Exodus 19:6

God's plan for His people is to serve as priests, to live as a holy nation.

A priest is a servant who ministers on behalf of God, a bridge between humans and God. In a sense, Israel was to be a priest to the whole world, building a bridge to the only true way of life.

And how were the people to do that? By being a holy nation. By living in light of God's truth. By being set apart from the empty ways of the world.

Today, the church serves in much the same way. At least, it's supposed to. But the church isn't a nation with physical boundaries. Its members infiltrate the world as a whole.

And as a believer, you are called to be a bridge builder to the world around you. Walking with your Lord, letting His light and truth and love shine through you. Today, if you look for them, you'll find ample opportunities to serve in just that way.

Warn the people that they are forbidden to touch any part of the mountain. Anyone who does will be put to death.

—Exodus 19:12

You can go too far. You can cross the line. And you can get in very serious trouble.

That was true when it came to approaching God. He had Moses set boundaries around the mountain of His presence to protect the people from His unyielding holy power. If they touched the mountain—even though it was mere rock, dirt, and vegetation—they would die.

Such is the power of God's holy purity. And it is a strong reminder of the importance of setting and keeping boundaries in life.

Not walls. Not barriers. But boundaries. Boundaries protect us and others from unhealthy behavior. There is a limit to what we can do for others and what they can do for us. There is a limit to our time, our energy, our abilities.

God protected His people from going too far. He will do the same for you.

Go and warn the people not to cross the boundary that you set at the foot of the mountain. They must not cross it to come and look at me, because if they do, many of them will die. Only the priests may come near me, and they must obey strict rules before I let them. If they don't, they will be punished.

—Exodus 19:21–22

God cannot be contained. Within His omnipresent being is the totality of holiness, power, and justice. To approach Him is to come into the presence of a purity that must annihilate any speck of sin. That was why He told Moses to warn the people that if they came to the mountain and gazed at Him, they would perish.

So how can we approach God? Yes. God has provided the way. He sent His sinless Son Jesus Christ to take our punishment on Himself. And now, in Christ, we can approach God in freedom and fullness.

I am the LORD your God, the one who brought you out of Egypt where you were slaves.

—Exodus 20:2

The agreement was cast. The covenant was shaped. And God's commands followed the form of an official agreement. God introduced Himself, validated Himself, and proved His love and care for the people.

There was no doubt who was behind the momentous events of the Exodus. It wasn't good luck. It wasn't the expert leadership skills of Moses or the weakness of Pharaoh. It was God. And He was exercising His rights over His people.

He had bought them. He owned them. He absolutely committed Himself to them. Most of all, He loved them as His children.

So He had every right—as their Creator, Sustainer, and Liberator—to establish their way of living. It was for their own good.

Who is God to you? What great acts has He performed in your life? How is He asking you to live in light of your relationship?

Do not worship any God except me.
—Exodus 20:3

At the time the Israelites lived, the world was full of gods. At least in the minds of the people of various nations. Each nation sported its own panoply of gods. Most of them were bloodthirsty and cruel. Most of them held their deluded subjects in terror. And still, the Israelites often flirted with such gods.

The one true God said, "Do not worship any god except me." The other gods were false—or worse, demonic. Who could even think of entertaining the notion of ignoring God and chasing after the wind like that?

Today, there are few competing gods. But there are many godlike things in our lives. Money. Possessions. Power. Pleasure. Success. Fame. Work. Relationships. And on and on. Everyone wrestles with one or more of them. Which ones do the most to keep your eyes off God Himself?

The first commandment God gave His people was to focus on Him exclusively. How well are you obeying Him today?

Do not make idols that look like anything in the sky or on earth or in the ocean under the earth. Don't bow down and worship idols.

—Exodus 20:4–5a

God is jealous. He wants the full allegiance of His children. And He is very careful to make sure we know that.

In the case of the Israelites, God spelled out that they were not to build or carve or form in any way a likeness to any living creature—or any creature of the imagination—to be an idol.

God wanted to spare His children the frustration and emptiness of worshiping an inanimate object that had no power. Serving such things was only a waste of time and energy. And that time and energy could be put to better use God's way.

God genuinely seeks our best and wants to protect us from harm and folly. If we would only look at it that way, obedience would be a pleasure.

I am the LORD your God, and I demand all your love. If you reject me, I will punish your families for three or four generations. But if you love me and obey my laws, I will be kind to your families for thousands of generations.

—*Exodus 20:5b–6*

God explains how He feels about the people on this earth. He divides us into those who reject Him and those who love Him. He jealously woos each soul to His side. But when the decision is made, the consequences accrue.

Those who reject Him get stuck in the mire of selfish wickedness—and that affects offspring for generations to come. Those who love Him, on the other hand, are privileged to bask in His mercy and love.

Yes, God is patient. Yes, God is forgiving. Yes, God will accept anyone who comes to Him. But at some point, there may be no turning back. Do you know anyone who needs to hear that today?

Do not misuse my name. I am the LORD your God, and I will punish anyone who misuses my name.

—Exodus 20:7

How frivolously God's name is uttered today! Just turn on your television, watch a movie, or listen to everyday conversation. In the mind of society, the power of the name of God diminishes. It's watered down with repeated use that's empty of meaning and devoid of connection to the almighty Ruler of the universe.

In light of that, this commandment is a rather startling indictment. Technically, it may refer to swearing by God's name that you'll do something when you actually have no intention of doing so. It's an empty promise, and attaching God's name to it only empties it of meaning as well.

You already know God is jealous for those He loves. He wants us to take Him seriously. And that includes His name. Realize how powerful that name can be for you today. Don't cheapen it with casual use; rather, revere it.

Remember that the Sabbath Day belongs to me. You have six days when you can do your work, but the seventh day of each week belongs to me, your God.

—Exodus 20:8–10a

God seems to hold a pretty strict line when it comes to Sabbath rest. And the Israelites did their best to follow it.

In fact, by Jesus' day, the Sabbath had become mired in all kinds of minute judgments. To the point that a good Jew could do barely more than just sit all day.

But God's command was not a restriction. Rather, it was an invitation. By giving us a day of rest, He invites us to take the time to think, pray, be. He invites us into His presence and into the fellowship of kindred souls in worship, learning, and meditation. And He invites us to spend time with ourselves.

Jesus said the Sabbath exists for us. It is for our own good—as are all the commandments. It is rest. Peace. Communion. Renewal. Fellowship.

Accept the invitation.

In six days I made the sky, the earth, the oceans, and everything in them, but on the seventh day I rested. That's why I made the Sabbath a special day that belongs to me.

—Exodus 20:11

God created everything in a certain amount of time, and then He rested.

He didn't *need* to rest. He wasn't tired. His fingers weren't sore from the work He'd done. His back wasn't aching. He took the time to stop, look at what He had accomplished, and consider it good. It was valuable to Him. So valuable, He wants us to do the same.

We all get weary from our week of activities. But the sabbath rest is not just about resting our bodies; it's about renewing our souls and recharging our spirits.

It's about thinking through our week: what we accomplished, what we have yet to do, where we failed, how we need to correct our steps. It's about meditating on God and our relationship with Him. Begin making a conscious effort to spend your Sabbath as God would have you spend it.

Respect your father and your mother, and you will live a long time in the land I am giving you.

—Exodus 20:12

What does this commandment mean, anyway? As a general rule, it means holding your parents in esteem. Caring for them. Obeying them while under their authority.

Parents are humans, too. They make mistakes. Sometimes they express themselves in harmful ways. Sometimes they expect too much of us. Still, knowing that, we are to respect and honor them. We are to realize the important role they play in our lives and prize that. We are to express our love as best we can for them.

That's the way God set up the human system. When we work within that system, we benefit, our parents benefit, and society benefits. And when we live in obedience to this commandment, our lives will be lengthened—at least in terms of fulfillment and richness.

How can you obey this commandment today?

Do not murder. Be faithful in marriage. Do not steal.

—Exodus 20:13–15

Three commandments we're all familiar with but conveniently put on the shelf because we're not murderers, adulterers, or thieves. Until we read Jesus' words in the Sermon on the Mount, and realize the very thought of murder, adultery, or theft is in effect a breach of the law.

We all sin. And that, as the New Testament tells us, is the whole point of the law: to show us our need for righteousness outside ourselves.

Jesus' intention in broadening the definition of murder, adultery, and theft was not to load unresolvable guilt upon us but to force us to look to Him for relief. In ourselves, we are incapable of obeying God's perfect law. With Jesus, we are holy, righteous, and pure in God's eyes.

In Him are forgiveness and cleansing. In Him is power to live healthy lives. In Him is the fulfillment of real life. And within His protective boundaries, stated in the law, are freedom and safety.

Do not tell lies about others.

—Exodus 20:16

On the face of this commandment is the admonition not to speak untruth in regard to others—untruth that would put them in jeopardy or cause them problems. But underneath this command is a call to live as an honest, transparent person. To understand your feelings and thoughts, and to express them appropriately to others.

Not to hold back truth that may hurt, but to express it carefully, honestly, and positively with a view to helping and building up the other person.

Not to protect yourself from negative feelings, but to recognize them and handle them in healthy ways.

Not to use words falsely to harm someone who has harmed you, but to confront that person with your true feelings and seek reconciliation.

Consider your words and actions today in light of this commandment. How would life be different if you obeyed God's command to speak the truth in love?

Do not want anything that belongs to someone else. Don't want anyone's house, wife or husband, slaves, oxen, donkeys or anything else.

—Exodus 20:17

Once again, God protects His children from harm. Without this commandment, our nature would force us to continually seek ways, things, and people in which to find fulfillment and joy. And that is simply impossible.

Paul urges us to be content in whatever state we're in (see Phil. 4:11). Contentment is finding fulfillment in what we have, what we are. It is resting in the knowledge that God has provided—and will provide—everything we need for life.

Be content. Know God. Accept His peace and provision.

Build an altar out of earth, and offer on it your sacrifices of sheep, goats, and cattle. Wherever I choose to be worshiped, I will come down to bless you.

—Exodus 20:24

The Lord God proscribes in general terms the means of worship He desires from His people: a simple altar of earth; sacrifices; acceptance of His blessings for obedience.

Humanity tends to make it much more complex than it needs to be. Ornate rituals, complex proceedings, layer upon layer of regulation. To the point that we focus so heavily on the apparatus that we can't see God.

God desires the heartfelt approach of a soul yearning to know Him. A soul that comes to Him through the one great sacrifice of the Lamb of God.

That's all it takes. If that simple approach to the altar of God is not the basis, you cannot reach Him.

Think of the ways you approach God. Are you accepting His gracious invitation to come in faithful simplicity?

DAY 88

Now these are the judgments which you shall set before them.

—Exodus 21:1 (NKJV)

God gave Moses a whole array of laws by which the nation of Israel should be governed. Every aspect of life was addressed, but the bottom line through it all was the same: justice and mercy.

In all their dealings, God's people were to treat others with fairness and understanding. But more, they were to live mercifully toward others. With grace, acceptance, deference, and honor. It's the way God deals with all His people. His way is right and perfect. And it is seasoned with grace and mercy.

The law was established for the good of the nation, to enable sinful human beings to approach a holy God and live in peace and order with one another.

Now we live according to the Spirit, who dwells within each of God's children. The law is written on our hearts rather than on stone tablets. It is a way of life that arises out of an obedient, growing relationship with God. But the basis is still the same: justice and mercy.

That is the way of life God desires in you. And He will empower you to fulfill it.

MARCH 28

But if [the woman] is seriously injured, the payment will be life for life, eye for eye, tooth for tooth, hand for hand, foot for foot.

—Exodus 21:23–24

An eye for an eye, a tooth for a tooth. Today, this principle can seem harsh. This law of retaliation doesn't seem to fit the concept of forgiveness and mercy.

And Jesus seemed to discount it in the Sermon on the Mount. He pointed to this law and said God's people were to turn the other cheek.

But God established this principle as a protective measure. It was intended not to promote retaliation, but to keep it in check. To limit the punishment for crime to what was fair and just.

The law of love, however, encourages us to respond to harm in the power of the Spirit. Not to be a weak, meek doormat, but to voluntarily set aside our rights. And only empowered people can set aside their rights for the glory of God.

That power is available to you today. Draw on it as you face confrontation and potential harm. Let Jesus use those situations to strengthen you even more.

Do not mistreat or abuse foreigners who live among you. Remember, you were foreigners in Egypt.

—Exodus 22:21

Of all people, the Israelites should know what it feels like to be strangers in the land. To dwell in a place that wasn't their own. To feel abandoned and alone, even lost in the world. To feel powerless over their circumstances and their destiny.

For over four hundred years they lived as slaves in Egypt. For forty more they wandered through the desert. In their own land, God instructed them to remember those feelings and treat others with understanding and compassion. Human nature made this a challenge. Inborn prejudice caused them to naturally look down upon those who were different.

Your world is filled with foreigners, or strangers. People who haven't found their "home" yet. People who have come from different parts of the world and who desire to be accepted and treated humanely.

Who are these people in your life? Identify them. Reach out to them. Pray for them. Take steps to make them feel less like strangers and more like neighbors.

Do not mistreat widows or orphans. If you do, they will beg for my help, and I will come to their rescue. In fact, I will get so angry that I will kill your men and make widows of their wives and orphans of their children.

—Exodus 22:22–24

Throughout the Bible, God says that widows and orphans hold a special place in His heart. And so He calls His people to treat them with care.

In biblical times, widows and orphans were cared for by the community. Like a large family, the community provided for their physical and emotional needs.

In the same way, the church is admonished to care for those who are lost and alone. They may not even technically be widows or orphans, but they need compassionate understanding, a helping hand, a listening ear, a caring heart.

Are you fulfilling this call of God on His people in your church community? Perhaps you know an individual who needs to be part of your extended family of support, love, and care.

Don't spread harmful rumors or help a criminal by giving false evidence.

—Exodus 23:1

God demands honesty. And to foster dishonesty to the detriment of others is to act as wicked people do.

Our words, our witness, are to be marked by truth. And until we know what is true, from every side of the story, we have no business spreading any report. It only causes harm. Not only to the subject of the report, but to us. Because it dissolves our integrity bit by bit.

You may have been on the hurt end of a false report. You know the sting of embarrassment and betrayal that you feel.

Don't fall into the trap of gossip. It is hurtful and dishonest. God demands the truth in every aspect of our lives.

You shall not follow a crowd to do evil; nor shall you testify in a dispute so as to turn aside after many to pervert justice.

—Exodus 23:2 (NKJV)

We find ourselves in all kinds of groups of people, at work, in our neighborhood, in our circle of acquaintances. We may not feel any strong attachment to these groups. But if they are not sourced in a relationship with God, we may find ourselves carried along into an activity or an attitude that is incompatible with His ways.

It can happen suddenly, unexpectedly. Before you know it, you've "followed the crowd" into something that is harmful to yourself or to others.

God encourages us to establish our boundaries, to know how far we should go to protect ourselves. So that when we come up against those boundaries, we'll have the strength to stand firm and disengage from the activity. And, if need be, from the group itself.

The mob mentality can be destructive. Guard your heart and your mind. Feed on the grace and justice of God, and let these qualities work through you to others.

If you find an ox or a donkey that has wandered off, take it back where it belongs, even if the owner is your enemy. If a donkey is overloaded and falls down, you must do what you can to help, even if it belongs to someone who doesn't like you.

—Exodus 23:4–5

Justice is always balanced with mercy in God's eyes. And in this word, you catch a sense of Jesus' admonition in the Sermon on the Mount to turn the other cheek, to walk the extra mile, to give your tunic as well as your cloak.

There will always be people with whom you disagree. People who don't understand you and who don't really want to.

But you are not to adopt their practices of division, destruction, and self-protection. God proposes something revolutionary: to reach out to them in concern; to help meet a need when you come across it; to take the initiative with a positive act.

God clearly instructed the Israelites to keep their boundaries up against their pagan enemies. He also called on them to help their enemies when the opportunity arose.

Our ability to do the same comes only from the strength of our boundaries. Keep your boundaries with the world strong so you can serve the world in God's power.

DAY 95

Each year bring the best part of your first harvest to
the place of worship.

—Exodus 23:19

God asked His people to dedicate to Him the
firstborn of every living creature and of every
family in the land. And He also asked for the first
part of the harvest of crops. They would be used
for various sacrifices, for service, for building the
relationship with God. And they would constantly remind the Israelites that God comes first.

The truth is, God possesses everything—not
just the first part. But by returning the first part
to Him, the Israelites acknowledged His authority over all.

Oftentimes, we get it backward. We fit our relationship with God into our already busy schedule. Whatever time or money or energy is left—if
any—that's what we offer to God.

What would happen if you recognized this
truth in your daily life? It just might change your
relationship with Him.

APRIL 4

DAY 96

I am sending an angel to protect you and to lead you into the land I have ready for you. Carefully obey everything the angel says, because I am giving him complete authority, and he won't tolerate rebellion.

—Exodus 23:20–21

God sent an angel to guide, protect, and watch over the people of Israel. And He meant business.

The angel came with the authority of God. With the judgment of God. With the name of God.

The angel was filled with God's presence. He revealed God's will. He uttered God's Word. And he offered God's protection and guidance.

God still sends His messenger angels to guide us and protect us. Perhaps their influence isn't as dramatic as this one—many scholars believe this was the preincarnate Christ.

Even so, His angels are active behind the scenes. We can't see them. But we can believe them. And we can thank God for them.

Come up on the mountain and stay here for a while.
I will give you the two flat stones on which I have
written the laws that my people must obey.

—*Exodus 24:12*

The first written words of God were meant to
be used. God called Moses into His presence on
the mountain to give him stone tablets on which
He had written the law.

Moses was to return to the people with them.
Not to show them off. Not to worship them. Not
to display them handsomely. But to teach them.

The Bible is designed to be read. Used.
Taught. Lived. Wrestled with. Communicated.
Followed. Debated. Figured out. Questioned.
Trusted. Loved.

Is that what you're doing with God's Word?

The only way to work the Word into your life
is first to read it. Immerse yourself in it. Study it.
Talk about it with other believers.

And the rest will flow out of that foundation.

Tell everyone in Israel who wants to give gifts that
they must bring them to you.

—Exodus 25:2

God established a complicated system of sacrifices to enable the people of Israel to come to
Him in holiness and acceptance. But above that,
God also encouraged voluntary contributions.
Money or possessions offered willingly. Materials
of all kinds with which to make a sanctuary and
decorate it fittingly.

Such offerings revealed a heart that truly loved
God and sought to serve Him wholeheartedly.
God would gladly accept such offerings and use
them not for His benefit, but for their own. For
with them they would construct a place where
they could meet with Him.

In truth, all our offerings are for our ultimate
benefit. No matter what we give, the body of
Christ prospers. And as part of that body, we
prosper in some way as well.

Knowing that is true can make our hearts even
more willing to give. We don't give to get. We
give to share, to honor God, to promote His
kingdom. And when that happens, we will receive far more than we could ever give.

I also want them to build a special place where I can live among my people. Make it and its furnishings exactly like the pattern I will show you.

—Exodus 25:8–9

God wanted His people to build a special place where they could go for quiet, for healing, for rest. For God's presence. It was to be a sanctuary—a holy place.

In the world we are surrounded by noise and lights. By responsibilities. By needs. By activities. We yearn for fresh air, clear skies, relaxed bodies, freedom. We want to feel heard and loved and cared for. We want to know God and be known by God. We want to worship.

There is a special place where all this can happen. Not the place the Israelites built to meet with God. Not even your church building—although that's a good place to go, too. This special place is right where you are, right now. Because right now, you are in the presence of God. Ask Him for what you need today.

DAY 100

I will meet you there between the two creatures and tell you what my people must do and what they must not do.

—Exodus 25:22

Imagine it. The God of the universe would lower Himself to enter a structure built with human hands in order to meet with His people. To hear them, love them, teach them.

Hundreds of years later, God would come to earth not in a handcrafted structure, but in the form of a human being. Jesus Christ. His purpose was the same: to hear us, love us, teach us.

Today, God comes to earth to dwell within each child of His. There He guides us, speaks to us, empowers us, teaches us.

You are a sanctuary for the presence of God. For He dwells within you.

Listen as He speaks to you today.

Aaron is to be dedicated as my high priest, and his clothes must be made only by persons who possess skills that I have given them.

—Exodus 28:3

God had gifted certain artisans so that they might create the priest's clothing. Their knowledge and abilities set them apart. They were equipped to make the finest quality garments.

Artistic gifts are a joy to exercise. Some people are specially endowed with abilities to do certain things—sing, draw, play an instrument, paint, compose music, cook, write prose or poetry.

You have certain gifts of creative expression, too. Perhaps you have yet to fully realize your God-given potential.

God can give you a special know-how to glorify Him with. If that's your desire, ask Him for it. If you haven't yet discovered your creative gift, try something new.

DAY 102

You and your descendants must always offer this sacrifice on the altar at the entrance to the sacred tent. People of Israel, I will meet and speak with you there, and my shining glory will make the place holy.

—Exodus 29:42–43

In the place God had established to meet with His people, an altar stood in the entryway. On that altar, sacrifices would be burned as offerings continually. And with this constant offering, there would always be a means for the Israelite to come into God's presence.

Today, there is no need for such sacrificial offerings. God does not require continual burnt offerings in order to come into His presence.

One single offering is all it took to open the door forever. One single offering gave us the power to come into God's presence as His sons and daughters. That was the offering by Jesus Christ of His own life. And when we accept that offering as given on our own behalf and put our trust in Him, we can always come into God's presence.

Once a year Aaron must purify the altar by smearing on its four corners the blood of an animal sacrificed for sin, and this practice must always be followed. The altar is sacred because it is dedicated to me.

—*Exodus 30:10*

The blood of atonement covered the nation's sins for the year. The practice had to be repeated every year throughout all their generations.

Always sinning, always covering it up. Never reaching perfect holiness. Always having to deal with the sins that separated them from God and each other. Forever and ever, it would never get better.

It can feel that way to us today, too. Continually we stretch forward, reaching for healthiness and righteousness. We work hard, we celebrate little victories, then we crash. We feel defeated. The goal seems so far away, and we feel so powerless to reach it.

We should know better by now, we think. We should be stronger, healthier. And we are. But the more we grow, the more we realize how much more growth is needed. Growth that God will gladly give us.

I have chosen Bezalel from the Judah tribe to make the sacred tent and its furnishings. Not only have I filled him with my Spirit, but I have given him wisdom and made him a skilled craftsman.

—*Exodus 31:2–3*

There was a lot of work to do. Construction of the ornate tabernacle, the ark of the covenant, the various altars and lavers and other materials.

Someone had to do the work. God appointed a man whom He had filled with His Spirit. And to accomplish His task, God endowed Bezalel with wisdom and craftsmanship.

Bezalel was uniquely equipped to carry out this God-given service. And that was but a foretaste of how God would work within His church.

Now, God dwells within *every* believer. He provides spiritual gifts to *every* believer. And He calls *every* believer to special service.

Today, examine your life, your interests, your desires. Ask God how He is calling you to serve Him in your own special way.

Hurry back down! Those people you led out of Egypt are acting like fools. They have already stopped obeying me.

—Exodus 32:7–8a

As God told Moses to return from the mountain to the people, He called them "*those* people *you* led out of Egypt." It was as though He washed His hands of them.

And why? Because they broke the first commandment. They created a calf god, worshiped it, sacrificed to it, and claimed it represented the god who had brought them out of Egypt.

Of course, we can't pin human emotions to the God of the universe. We could never fully understand His reasons, His emotions, His plans.

The truth that this word reveals, however, is God's jealousy. He wants to keep us for Himself. He wants us to know Him, trust Him, love Him wholeheartedly.

And He is hurt when we don't. He desires our solid allegiance.

I'm angry enough to destroy them, so don't try to stop me. But I will make your descendants into a great nation.

—*Exodus 32:10*

God established a covenant with the people of Israel. All He asked was that they serve Him. And they broke that covenant by worshiping a piece of metal they had formed in the shape of a calf.

God was angry with them. He was ready to wipe them out and start all over again with Moses, creating a whole new nation from him.

Obviously, that was just one option. For God still loved His people. All it took was one person, Moses, to plead with God to change His mind and spare the harm He intended to wreak on the people.

And God did relent. He was willing to keep working with the stubborn people. Until they got it right.

Thank God, He is just as patient with us, too.

It is a land rich with milk and honey. . . . I would go with my people, but they are so rebellious that I would destroy them before they get there.

—Exodus 33:2–3

The promise stood. The land of milk and honey awaited the coming of the people of Israel. But God remained angry with them. In fact, He sent them on their way alone—with only the angel going before them. For if He had accompanied them—if He had been in their presence for one moment—He was liable to wipe them out for their rebelliousness.

The people responded with mourning. God had gotten through to them with the gravity of their situation.

Ultimately, God would judge their rebellion. But not before He offered them opportunity after opportunity to return to Him.

God's resources of patience are vast, but not infinite. You can count on Him to accept you back into His arms time after time—up to a point. Then you may begin to suffer the consequences of your actions. Wouldn't you rather walk with God than walk alone? His hand is extended to you now.

The LORD would speak to Moses face to face, just like a friend.

—Exodus 33:11

This verse isn't a quotation of God's words, but it reveals His heart's desire for relating to His children. Think about the words. Imagine how Moses must have felt, basking in the presence of God, communing intimately with Him, face-to-face. Just as you would speak to your friend.

Isn't that your desire, too? Then make it happen. Sit comfortably in a quiet place free of distractions. You can even lie on the floor or take a walk. But simply talk.

Tell God what's on your heart. The pains, the frustrations, the fears, the hopes, the joys, the sorrows. Bring them all up to Him, and lay them before Him. Tell Him about them as you would your most intimate friend.

Then listen. You may not hear words. You may feel feelings, see pictures, get impressions, or remember a Bible verse. Listen to God in all of that. And let the conversation continue.

I will go with you and give you peace.
—Exodus 33:14

Moses spoke to God from his heart, honestly and directly. His frustration bubbled over: "I know that you have told me to lead these people to the land you promised them. But you have not told me who my assistant will be. You have said that you are my friend and that you are pleased with me. If this is true, let me know what your plans are, then I can obey and continue to please you. And don't forget that you have chosen this nation to be your own" (vv. 12–13).

God answered with words that were comforting and promising. God would be with him on the way. And He would give Moses peace.

Don't play games when it comes to talking to God. Don't hold back. Ask Him for what you need. And then trust Him to answer in the best way possible.

DAY 110

I will do what you have asked, because I am your
friend and I am pleased with you.

—Exodus 33:17

Moses persuaded God with the power of his
honesty and directness. By proving his allegiance
to God, Moses received God's promise to be with
him. But Moses asked for more: not just that
God would accompany him, but that He would
accompany the whole nation of Israel as well.

Moses' compassion for his people had an impact on God. He agreed to do what Moses asked
"because I am your friend." Theirs was a special
relationship, deep and strong and unshakable.
And Moses' commitment and closeness to God
were bathed in His grace and acceptance.

That's the same kind of relationship every believer can enjoy with God today. It's as real and
meaningful as any relationship could be. And it
will never, ever end.

It takes time to develop a relationship like
that. Time in communicating, in reading His
Word, in being with Him. But that's time spent
the very best way possible.

APRIL 19

I am the LORD, and I show mercy and kindness to anyone I choose. I will let you see my glory and hear my holy name.

—Exodus 33:19

Moses yearned to see God. He wanted some kind of physical manifestation of God's transcendence. But God cannot be boxed into our perception of what He should be. He is too infinite for that to happen.

Still, God did what He could to meet Moses' need. He permitted Moses to take a brief glance at His back as He passed by.

In describing to Moses what would happen, God noted His sovereignty in His dealings with humanity. It is His choice to shed mercy and kindness on us. He is the final authority in the universe, and there is no questioning that.

Having experienced God's mercy and kindness, you can draw comfort from the knowledge that He chose to share those qualities with you. And someday, you will see Him face-to-face. And bask in His glory forever.

DAY 112

I am the LORD God. I am merciful and very patient with my people. I show great love, and I can be trusted. I keep my promises to my people forever, but I also punish anyone who sins. When people sin, I punish them and their children, and also their grandchildren and great-grandchildren.

—Exodus 34:6–7

To a nation still wounded by God's anger over their idolatrous sin, His words must have seemed incredibly balming and deeply encouraging. God is full of mercy. Full of patience. Full of love. Full of forgiveness.

He cleanses all sin—every wrong thing we could commit. That is, as long as we ask for it.

You see, those who don't repent will be destroyed. And the consequences of their sins can even affect their descendants.

God's abounding mercy and love were music to the ears of the hurting Israelites. Perhaps His words can be the same for you today.

Behold, I make a covenant. Before all your people I will do marvels such as have not been done in all the earth, nor in any nation; and all the people among whom you are shall see the work of the LORD. For it is an awesome thing that I will do with you.

—Exodus 34:10 (NKJV)

God reiterated His agreement with the nation of Israel. He promised to do amazing things in their midst—miracles that had never been done anywhere before. And all the neighboring peoples would see the miraculous works of God.

God seemed to delight in His promise. It was as though He couldn't wait to show them His stuff. He couldn't wait to see the amazed expressions on the faces of the Israelites and their neighbors when they saw what happened. And it would be like nothing they had ever seen.

That's the kind of God you know today. Creative, powerful, eager to work in your life. Delighting in His ability to surprise you with amazing works.

What would you ask Him for? How would you like to be surprised?

And how would you like to surprise God?

Don't make treaties with any of those people. If you do, it will be like falling into a trap.

—Exodus 34:12

The people who already lived in the land God had given the Israelites were dangerous. And as history unfolds through the Scriptures, you can see why.

Their pagan religions kept enticing God's people. And their sinful predilections attracted the Israelites as well. The forces of evil were so powerful that, ultimately, the nation of Israel would disintegrate in the poison of sin with which their neighbors had infected them.

God said, be careful. Something that would look good and honorable on the surface—a treaty of peace with other peoples, allowing them to cohabit in the land—would ultimately be a trap. And Israel would lose.

Sound like the world you live in? Often arrangements with this world may look good, but they may pull you down into activities you may not have even imagined. Beware. Trust God. And then you can venture out into the land.

If the animal is a bull, it must not have anything wrong with it. Lead it to the entrance of the sacred tent, and I will let you know if it is acceptable to me.
—*Leviticus 1:3*

In the book of Leviticus, God outlined the various sacrifices and offerings that enabled His people to come into His presence.

In the agrarian economy of Israel, male animals were worth more, and they signified strength and vitality. And the animals offered were to have no defects. In other words, the offerings were valuable.

As we read of the various offerings in Leviticus, we may be amazed. The concept seems so foreign to us. Imagine approaching God daily through the offering of an animal on an altar of fire.

God has made other provisions for us: the once and for all sacrifice of His Son Jesus Christ. It is His desire to allow us into His presence, and He has made the way clear. All we need to do is walk in it.

DAY 116

Lay your hand on its head, and I will accept the animal as a sacrifice for taking away your sins.

—Leviticus 1:4

The burnt offerings were a means by which God's people could approach Him in His holiness. And that was made evident by placing one's hand on the head of the animal.

This act marked the identification of the Israelite with the sacrifice. The death of the animal was accepted as covering for the sin of the individual.

When we think of Jesus' sacrifice on the cross, we often note that He carried the sins of the whole world upon Him. We weren't there on Calvary to place a hand on Him as our sacrifice. But the fact remains that He identified with us. Every one of us.

He took upon Himself every sin we have ever and will ever commit. And Christ's death was effective for all sins forever.

He paid the penalty for your sins personally. And now, because of that, He can take your hand in fellowship and walk with you day by day.

Instead of a bull or a cow, you may offer any sheep or goat that has nothing wrong with it.

—*Leviticus 3:6*

This verse describes a peace offering, which opened the door to experiencing fellowship with God. The name *peace offering* is related to the Hebrew word *shalom,* which means "peace" or "wholeness." And that was God's desire for His people.

He cleared the way to enable them to experience peace between Himself and them. And that kind of relationship results in a sense of true peace within the soul.

This is true fellowship with God. With this offering, the believer—as well as the priest—was allowed to eat part of the sacrifice. It was as though they were sharing a meal with a friend. And the friend was God Himself.

God still desires to fellowship with His children as friends at a meal (see Rev. 3:20). No sacrifices are needed now, other than your time and effort. But that's a sacrifice well worth making.

DAY 118

Offer a sacrifice to ask forgiveness when you sin by
accidentally doing something I have told you not to
do. . . . When the high priest sins, he makes everyone else guilty too. And so, he must sacrifice a young
bull that has nothing wrong with it.

—Leviticus 4:2–3

When a person—or even a priest—broke a
commandment of God in ignorance, without realizing that it was a transgression, God made
provision for a sin offering to restore the relationship with Him.

Unlike some of the other sacrifices, which
were voluntary, this one was required. Because
God deeply desired to maintain His relationship
with His people. But that was possible only when
sin was dealt with. Even unintentional sin.

That's why it's important to keep your spiritual senses open to God's leading within you. Ask
Him to examine your heart and reveal hidden
hurts, sins, attitudes, or behaviors that can keep
you from walking closely with Him. Open your
heart to His healing work.

Now if the whole congregation of Israel sins unintentionally, and the thing is hidden from the eyes of the assembly . . . ; when the sin which they have committed becomes known, then the assembly shall offer a young bull for the sin, and bring it before the tabernacle of meeting.

—Leviticus 4:13–14 (NKJV)

The sin of the individual. The sin of the religious leader. The sin of the congregation as a whole. Each type of sin made an impact on the history of Israel. And we see God make provision for dealing with it in every aspect.

We see it all played out in our own day as well. Individual sin we can understand—we're merely human. The sin of religious leaders is troubling, but we can understand the corruption of power at work in the lives of sinful humans.

The sin of the congregation as a whole—from apathy to rebellion—is much more troubling because it is often committed without realization. And for an entire congregation to deal with its sin is like turning a battleship—it takes time and great effort to change course. But today, God's Spirit is able to revive the hearts of those involved.

You are guilty the moment you realize that you have made a hasty promise to do something good or bad.
—Leviticus 5:4

The words of our mouths are powerful. They not only affect others but ourselves. In a moment of anger, we may utter hurtful words. At other times, we may even say things that seem good and helpful but are not sourced in the truth of God and are therefore ultimately damaging.

You've no doubt had the experience of having your words come back to haunt you. You may make a promise, share some advice, anticipate the future, speak out of time, cross some healthy boundaries. And then later you learn how those words hurt others, led them astray, or were more than they could handle.

Search your heart today in the light of God's Spirit. Open yourself up to His leading. Ask God if your words have harmed another. And if so, seek him or her out to clear the air. Make that part of your ongoing spiritual life.

As soon as you discover that you have committed any of these sins, you must confess what you have done.

—Leviticus 5:5

God listed to Moses a number of potential infractions. Then He called on His people to confess them when they realized their guilt.

In the Protestant church, we often shy away from the act of confession. It's easy to confess to God, but much more hurtful to our pride to confess to another. And yet, with sin that has deep roots in us, merely realizing it in ourselves and confessing it to God don't seem to clear our consciences.

The New Testament encourages believers to confess sins one to another. Not necessarily before the entire congregation—although in some cases that may be necessary. Do you have a close brother or sister in the Lord with whom you can be totally honest?

God offers freedom. He desires fellowship. Don't let sin hinder your experience of joy and wholeness. Make your confession.

If you break any of my commands without meaning to, you are still guilty, and you can be punished.

—Leviticus 5:17

Maybe you've been pulled over in your car by a police officer for a traffic violation you didn't even know was a violation. You didn't have a clue you were doing anything wrong, but you had to pay a fine for it.

You can beg for mercy because you just didn't know. But that probably won't influence the police officer. Because ignorance of the law is no defense.

The Israelites may have had the same feelings with God. The Old Testament is filled with complex laws and regulations that few people could keep straight. Yet God stated that if you sin, you're guilty, whether you know you've broken the law or not.

God is holy, and He cannot tolerate sin. So when we realize we are off the path He has set for us, we should respond with heartfelt humility and repentance.

DAY 123

You have sinned if you rob or cheat someone, if you keep back money or valuables left in your care, or if you find something and claim not to have it. When this happens, you must return what doesn't belong to you.

—Leviticus 6:2–4

Those who stole or borrowed and lost or found something someone else had lost are responsible to restore what was taken. It may be a physical item. Or it may be more psychological.

Sometimes people steal others' joy, confidence, or security. Sometimes people are hurt by abandonment, abuse, or unconcern.

Perhaps you've had a role in creating that situation in another's life through your behavior. When you discover the wrong and how it happened, when you realize the role you played in "stealing" something from someone else, God says you are responsible to make restitution. That can be a courageous—and freeing—act.

The altar fire must always be kept burning—it must never go out.

—Leviticus 6:13

God mandated that the Israelites keep a fire on the altar at all times. It was never to go out. It represented a constant coming to God through the sacrifices. A constant connection with God. A continual dependency on God. An unbreakable bond of light and heat and life with God.

In Israel, that fire eventually burned out. And the people suffered the consequences.

Now the fire is within your soul. It blazes at times, smolders at others. But in Jesus Christ, it will never be extinguished.

Still, you must do your part to keep it burning. You must keep the drafts open to ensure it gets sufficient spiritual oxygen. You must keep the fuel coming through prayer, fellowship, Scripture meditation, learning, growing. You must stir the embers daily, adding more fuel, fanning the flames in the Spirit.

Stay near the entrance to the sacred tent until the ordination ceremony ends seven days from now.

—Leviticus 8:33

When Aaron was ordained and consecrated as the priest over Israel, serving as the intermediary between God and His people, he and his sons performed a series of rites and sacrifices as a form of dedication.

Part of the ordination involved staying inside the tabernacle—the place of the presence of God—for seven days. There God worked on their souls, loosing their sins, freeing them from life's baggage, empowering them, loving them.

Spending seven days in God's presence is a foreign concept to us. Yes, Aaron was called to a special task. And it would require huge reserves of emotional, spiritual, and physical strength. Strength only God could give.

We feel we do well to spend a half hour in God's presence each day. How can you enlarge your opportunities and expand your time with God?

I demand respect from my priests, and I will be
praised by everyone!

—Leviticus 10:3

Aaron's oldest sons took it upon themselves to
approach God on their own terms, offering incense God hadn't authorized.

Their act was not in God's will. And to show
the import of coming to God on His terms, God
consumed them with fire.

Tragic and shocking deaths. But they made an
impact on the nation. For God made it clear that
people could approach Him only in perfect holiness, or He must consume them.

We come to God on His terms. In His way.
For His glory. Not ours.

As believers today, we come to Him perfect
and forgiven and cleansed in Jesus Christ. We
have no fear of being consumed by fire. No fear
of not being accepted. Because His Son opened
the way for us to approach God in freedom and
confidence.

When you or your sons enter the sacred tent, you must never drink beer or wine. If you do, you will die right there! This law will never change.

—Leviticus 10:9

Aaron's position was of such importance that God stressed that he—and his sons—must be fully aware of what they were doing every moment. To protect them from His holy wrath, God instructed Aaron not to drink alcohol. Perhaps it had been instrumental in Aaron's sons' poor decisions—and outright rebellion—which led to death.

Coming to God is serious business. He requires our undivided attention. He desires our utter devotion. So anything that inhibits us or keeps us from entering in fully with Him is dangerous. Even our attitudes.

God wants us to enter into His presence fully aware, fully open, fully prepared to meet Him and receive from Him. That calls for total awareness.

I am the LORD your God, and you must dedicate
yourselves to me and be holy, just as I am holy.

—Leviticus 11:44a

These words about being holy are not a threat
or a standard God has set for us that's impossible
to achieve.

No, they are an invitation. God invites His
people to be His people. By choice. Fully. Deter-
minedly.

God desired His people Israel to be totally
consecrated. Set apart. Distinctive. He wanted
them to shine in a dark world. To stand out from
the mass of humanity that was stuck in the mire
of sin and self-will.

And He had every right to expect total devotion. Not only had He rescued them and provided for them, but He was God. And that is
enough.

He wants us to be the same. Dedicated. Determined. Desiring to be what He has called us
to be. Holy. Clean in Christ. Distinctive. Real.
And shining in a world that yearns for true light.

There you will lay your hands on [the live goat's] head, while confessing every sin the people have committed, and you will appoint someone to lead the goat into the desert, so that it can take away their sins.

—Leviticus 16:21

Scapegoat. Someone—or something—to lay the blame on. To take the heat.

In Israel's case, it was a literal goat, upon which Aaron placed all the sins of the children of God. Then it was sent away into the wilderness. There, presumably, to die. And Israel would perform this ritual every year.

Jesus is our eternal scapegoat. On Him, once for all, we have placed our trust. On Him were laid our sins and failures.

Your sins have been paid for by His death, yet the sins you commit form a barrier to fellowship between you and God. Once you placed your faith in Him for eternal salvation, but moment by moment you come to Him in confession, to seek His cleansing and His power. Is now such a moment?

This is the day on which the sacrifice for the forgiveness of your sins will be made in my presence, and from now on, it must be celebrated each year. Go without eating and make this a day of complete rest just like the Sabbath.

—Leviticus 16:30–31

Every year, on the Day of Atonement, Israel offered up her sins for God's cleansing. It was a deeply painful, brutally honest, utterly solemn occasion. But it led to a cleansed life. So it was worth the pain, the honesty, and the solemnity.

How clean do you feel right now? The stresses of life have your nerves raw. The pains of the past gnaw at your sense of completion. The emptiness of life enlarges your neediness to the point of drowning at times. And all that leads you down the path of temptation. And perhaps into the mire of sin.

Imprint the concept of God's cleansing on you. Take a shower or a bath, and as you do, confess the barriers you've erected between you and God. Then accept His inner cleansing.

Life is in the blood, and I have given you the blood
of animals to sacrifice in place of your own.

—Leviticus 17:11

The blood of the sacrifice was holy. The animal
gave its very life to enable God's people to enter
into His presence.

The blood shed enabled the people of God to
make atonement for their souls. To be "at one"
with God through the principle of life for life.

We can sorrow over the animals that were
slain, or we can rejoice that God made a way for
humanity. We can grieve over the death of the
very Son of God, or we can rejoice that He rose
again in triumph, having paid the price for all to
enter God's presence in holiness and righteousness.

Life is sacred to God. So sacred that He was
willing to give some of it up in order to enable
many more to experience life more fully.

Your life is sacred to God. He has paid dearly
to have you live with Him forever. Is your life sacred to you? Are you spending it wisely?

Obey [my teachings] and you will live. I am the
LORD.

—Leviticus 18:5

Do's and don'ts. Rigid rights and wrongs. Does
your soul cringe at those words?

You yearn for a living, breathing faith that
moves and doubts and cries and praises and
grows stronger. You yearn to grow into the truth
by confronting the false in your life. You yearn to
courageously step into the will of God, seeking
to know Him and serve Him.

So how can the rules and regulations set forth
help you do all that? Don't they inhibit your freedom, imprison your spirit, deaden your life?

No. Not God's way. In fact, God says you will
live fully and boldly in God's power if you obey.

We are accepted by God not because of what
we do but because of who we are. His Word
shows us how to live in peace. With Him, with
others, and with ourselves. And that is the most
fulfilling life there is.

Don't make yourselves unclean by any of these disgusting practices of those nations that I am forcing out of the land for you. They made themselves and the land so unclean, that I punished the land because of their sins, and I made it vomit them up.

—Leviticus 18:24–25

God told the Israelites about the behaviors that offended His holiness. They were the behaviors that the nations inhabiting the land committed—degrading acts that brought His punishment upon them. To the point that the land would vomit out those inhabitants, enabling the Israelites to enter and dwell there.

God took the land and wiped it clean. And brought in new life in the form of the nation Israel.

In the same way, God acts in your life. You may have even experienced some of the behaviors God decries. In His power and grace, He can clean them out and refill you with new life. Come into the cleansed land, and live.

When you harvest your grain, always leave some of it standing along the edges of your fields and don't pick up what falls on the ground. Don't strip your grapevines clean or gather the grapes that fall off the vines. Leave them for the poor and for those foreigners who live among you. I am the LORD your God.

—Leviticus 19:9–10

God gave His people a command to provide for poor and needy people in a simple way: When reaping a field of grain, leave some standing. When gleaning grapes from the vineyard, leave some on the vine.

That way poor people could meet their own need from what was available. They could care for themselves out of the abundance of the fields.

The Israelites weren't instructed to harvest all the grain and give some away. The poor were expected to do what they needed to care for themselves. But God ensured that what they needed would be available.

Today, make an inventory of what you don't need. Food, clothing, toys, other possessions languishing in cupboards, closets, and garages. Unused, unappreciated, unneeded. Gather it together. Call your church or a homeless shelter to find out how best to distribute it to the needy.

I am the LORD your God, and I command you not to make fun of the deaf or to cause a blind person to stumble.

—Leviticus 19:14

God says, don't make life more difficult for people who must live with a disability. Instead, fear God.

Understand His heart. Tap in to His passion for people who are hurting. Be available to Him so He can work through you to build up rather than tear down.

We will always have physically, economically, and emotionally deprived people in our midst. We can choose to ignore them or, worse, to punish them for their situation.

Or we can choose to fear God and love them. To be a channel for His compassion toward them in constructive ways.

We can choose to communicate love to hearing impaired people and clear the path of any stumbling blocks for people who are blind.

Be fair, no matter who is on trial—don't favor either
the poor or the rich.

—Leviticus 19:15

As strong as His heart beats for poor and needy
people, God also cautioned His people to maintain fairness. Just because a person is poor is no
reason to ignore his wrongdoing or to excuse his
sin. Injustice performed by a needy person is still
injustice. And just because a person is wealthy or
powerful is no reason to let her have her way if
that way is unjust. She is responsible for her actions just as anyone else is.

The point is, sin is sin no matter who commits
it. One's economic or political standing should
have no sway when it comes to determining justice.

God's justice is pure and righteous and perfect
in every way. You can strive toward righteousness
in all your judgments as well. That starts by looking at the person as a person, and the act as an
act. And that can be done only in God's power
and wisdom.

Don't make yourselves disgusting to me by going to people who claim they can talk to the dead.

—*Leviticus 19:31*

God's jealousy of His people is evident once again. He called His people to avoid contact with those who claimed to be channels to the spirit world. Dealing with them would lead only to defilement and confusion.

You may scoff, comforting yourself with the thought that you'd never pay Madame Rene a visit for a palm reading. And yet, you may read the daily horoscope in your newspaper—just for the fun of it. Or you may read a book or watch a movie concerning demons or the netherworld—just for laughs. And those seemingly innocuous contacts could gradually dissolve your boundaries without your realizing it.

God calls His people to keep the fortifications strong. A fierce battle rages on the other side of reality. God has everything you need and more. There is no need to keep searching.

I command you to show respect for older people and
to obey me with fear and trembling.

—Leviticus 19:32

To the young, the older seem out of touch, unable to keep up. But as we grow older, we realize the strength, encouragement, and wisdom we can gain by interacting with older men and women.

They've been through life already. They can offer insights we couldn't imagine on our own. They may not have answers, but they have compassion. Because they understand the struggles we've been through with our jobs, our families, our spiritual journeys.

They can cheer us on. Their genuineness can give us hope. Their wisdom can give us patience as we continue to move through life. And their merry hearts can lighten the load.

God calls His people to show respect for those who are older. To learn from them and give them their due. Not only your family members, but those in your church or community.

Don't mistreat any foreigners who live in your land. Instead, treat them as well as you treat citizens and love them as much as you love yourself. Remember, you were once foreigners in the land of Egypt. I am the LORD your God.

—Leviticus 19:33–34

The Israelites knew what it felt like to be foreigners in a strange land. And after they were "home," they were to keep that understanding in mind when dealing with people who struggled with the same feelings.

It's easy to feel lost even in familiar circumstances. You may be feeling it right now.

Reach out to someone you can trust and tell him or her how you feel. Somewhere, there are people who have accepted God's call to reach out to "foreigners." And He will lead you to them at the right time.

Trust Him. And trust the process He is taking you through to rebuild your roots.

Use honest scales and don't cheat when you weigh or measure anything. I am the LORD your God. I rescued you from Egypt.

—Leviticus 19:35–36

In Israel, there was no government bureau with standards of weights and measures. It was everyone for himself or herself. So cheating was rampant. It wasn't difficult to shortchange a purchaser. And everyone did it. It was expected.

But God's standards were brought to bear. Every weight and measure was to be full. If not overflowing.

The Israelites were to live and work with justice—God's justice—in mind. They were to give what they were paid to give, fully and completely. Because that reflected the character of the God they served.

That may be a good reminder for you on the job today. Giving your employer a full hour's work for an hour's pay. Being honest with a customer without being compelled by government regulations and disclaimers. Going the extra mile in serving others.

Let His spirit of justice and righteousness permeate your dealings with others.

I have chosen certain times for you to come together
and worship me.

—Leviticus 23:2

God outlined for Israel a whole calendar of
feasts, times when the people were called together to celebrate various events of importance.

They offered rest for people, animals, and the
land. They recalled great events in history, such
as the deliverance from Egypt. They afforded an
opportunity to renew their dedication to the
Lord and to cleanse their sins.

In much the same way, we celebrate Thanksgiving, Christmas, Easter, and other special days.
They are times when family and friends can
gather together around a table to celebrate, share,
and remember.

In our world, such days can get lost in a lot of
secular hoopla. It's easy to lose sight of the sa-
credness of such days. Let this year be different
for you. Realize anew the meaning of each
"feast." Share it with your family and friends.
Use the day as an opportunity to grow closer to
God for what He has done.

This is a time of complete rest just like the Sabbath, and everyone must go without eating from the evening of the ninth to the evening of the tenth.
—*Leviticus 23:32*

God desired the company of His chosen people. So He arranged for them to atone for their sins through a deeply meaningful ceremony on a single day every year.

It was the only day God called His people to fast. The only day the great high priest entered the Holy of Holies in the tabernacle to atone for the people's sins. It was a day of intense introspection, grieving, and celebrating. It was a day set apart for the Lord. For dealing with sin. For getting right with Him.

We don't observe a single Day of Atonement today. Our atonement was made by Christ on the cross. And yet, in our soul of souls, every day is a Day of Atonement. A day to soberly address our faults, to yearn for God's cleansing, to seek His fellowship free of the burdens that weigh us down. A day to open ourselves to His power and will in our lives.

DAY 143

You may raise grain and grapes for six years, but the seventh year you must let your fields and vineyards rest in honor of me, your LORD.

—*Leviticus 25:3–4*

God had ordained a Sabbath every seventh day for people to rest. But the principle was expanded to the land as well.

Every seventh year, the Israelites were to leave the land to rest and replenish itself. That way it wouldn't lose its nutrients, and crops could flourish. Of course, the land would still produce food on its own. And that would be provision enough for the people, the servants, and the animals.

God would provide in His own way. And part of that provision was to allow the land to work itself without human intervention.

God in His wisdom knew the need for His creation to experience rest. To stop *doing* and just *be*. And then, the doing that followed would be that much more productive. How can you instill that principle into your life this week?

This fiftieth year is sacred—it is a time of freedom
and of celebration when everyone will receive back
their original property, and slaves will return home
to their families.

—Leviticus 25:10

God had already established a Sabbath of years
for the land. And every seventh seven-year period
was capped by a year of Jubilee. Land ownership
reverted to the original families. Slaves were set
free. The entire year was set aside for the celebration.

It was a time for the merry-go-round to stop,
so the people could get off, get back to basics, restore their roots, and start over fresh.

Our culture doesn't work like that. The concept would devastate the economy.

But God can still make all things new. He can
give a fresh start. At least internally. He can free
your heart from the ties that bind. And with a
new heart, you can pursue His will without hindrance.

If you obey my laws and teachings, you will live
safely in the land and enjoy its abundant crops.
—Leviticus 25:18–19

God had given the Israelites everything they
needed for successful living. It was give-and-take.
If the people would observe His commands—
care for the land, treat one another with dignity,
and serve Him—the land would be its own reward.

A look ahead in the Old Testament, however,
shows how shortsighted the Israelites were. They
continually broke God's commands and shunned
His way of life. And ultimately, they would be
forced to leave their land of safety, of provision.

God has stated what we need to do today to
maintain our growth, to walk in strength. And
we can be as willfully disobedient as they were.

What if we stopped demanding our own way?
We wouldn't lose ourselves, as we fear. We would
gain ourselves. We would experience security and
provision in every area of life.

DAY 146

Faithfully obey my laws, and I will send rain to make your crops grow and your trees produce fruit.

—*Leviticus 26:3–4*

Lord God, where is the blessing?

Where is the refreshing rain of cleansing, the rushing torrents of Your power, the fruit of Your Spirit in my life?

Why does my soul seem so dry, my spirit so desolate? Why do I continually thirst for Your presence? Why do You withhold what I yearn for?

Why do I struggle so hard to open the door of my heart to You? Why do I stand so defiantly against Your will?

Lord God, I desire to walk with You. But I know I want to walk on my own terms. And that is getting me nowhere. When will I acknowledge that? When will I surrender to Your power?

Can I do that now? Will I do that now?

I will bless your country with peace, and you will rest without fear. I will wipe out the dangerous animals and protect you from enemy attacks.

—Leviticus 26:6

God holds back until we are ready. Until we are willing to accept the great rush of blessings He desires to flood us with.

And He wants to do so much for His children. In the case of the Israelites, He yearned to give them peace in their land. Security. Safety. Freedom from fear. Rest.

Do you feel peace? Do you even remember what it feels like? Can you imagine life without the threat of failure or injury or abandonment or pain?

Peace is in the hands of God. And it can be yours when you climb into His arms.

The invitation is extended. His arms are wide open.

Open your eyes. Open you heart. Open your arms to Him.

DAY 148

You will chase and destroy your enemies, even if there are only five of you and a hundred of them, or only a hundred of you and ten thousand of them.

—Leviticus 26:7–8

In God's power, anything is possible.

Israel proved that many times. Their small band of ill-equipped soldiers often routed more powerful opponents. Larger, better equipped armies fell like straw men.

It wasn't that the Israelite soldiers were smarter, bigger, or luckier. God was with them. They carried out His purposes. His power worked through them.

It's unlikely you'll be called on to do physical battle. But you engage the enemy frequently. Every day. In many ways.

You don't have the power or the resources in yourself to outwit your enemies. But you do have the power of God available to you. Put on the armor of God (see Eph. 6). And then join the battle.

DAY 149

I am the LORD your God, and I rescued you from Egypt, so that you would never again be their slaves. I have set you free; now walk with your heads held high.

—Leviticus 26:13

Freedom. Broken shackles. Shattered yokes. Severed bonds.

The Israelites were slaves. And God completely freed them, removed them from the land of their captivity, and gave them a home.

You were a slave to sin. In Christ, the bonds have been broken. You have been set free. You walk uprightly.

And yet, you still feel shackled. The freedom you seek is elusive. You reach for it and get jerked back by harsh ropes of slavery.

You try. You work hard to loosen the shackles that still hold you.

But there is one key that opens the lock. It is the power of God.

Stop trying so hard to do it yourself. Do it in the power and wisdom of God. In His way, in His time, in His will, you can experience true freedom.

MAY 28

DAY 150

Your land will become so desolate that even your enemies who settle there will be shocked when they see it. After I destroy your towns and ruin your land with war, I'll scatter you among the nations.

—Leviticus 26:32–33

God outlined the consequences that would befall the Israelites if they did not obey Him. And it was not a pretty picture.

The land would become so desolate that even Israel's enemies would be dumbfounded. The people would be scattered, running at the point of a sword. Nothing would be left.

And that was exactly what happened, for precisely the reason God warned them about.

A disobedient heart leads only to emptiness and destruction.

God deeply desires His children to love and seek Him with their whole hearts. To follow Him, to walk with Him, to know Him.

If you humbly confess what you have done and start living right, I'll keep the promise I made to your ancestors. . . . I will bless your land.

—Leviticus 26:41–42

God forecast the desolation that Israel would suffer for disobedience. It was devastating to consider. And yet, He held out hope. There was still an out.

If the Israelites would repent—change their hearts and their minds toward God—and humble themselves before God and acknowledge their rebellion against Him, He would restore them. He would remember His promise to them. He would be their God once again.

Yes, God is a God of justice and righteousness. He desires His children to be with Him and walk with Him and obey Him.

But He is also a God of grace. Forgiveness. Cleansing. He is a God of new beginnings and fresh faith. And He is your God.

No matter what you have done, I am still the LORD your God, and I will never completely reject you or become absolutely disgusted with you there in the land of your enemies.

—Leviticus 26:44

Even though the people of God would ignore Him and pursue their own sinful lusts, their own self-centered ways, their own deluded priorities . . .

Even though God would judge their rebellion and scatter them to the land of their enemies . . .

Even though all would look lost forever, God would never sever His relationship with His people. He would not break His promise to them. Because He was the Lord their God. Forever and ever, amen. And it could only get better.

Our stubborn wills can get us into a lot of trouble. And we will suffer the natural and spiritual consequences of forcing our own sinful choices. But God understands. And He waits patiently for our return.

DAY 153

Marching behind Reuben will be the Levites, arranged in groups, just as they are camped. They will carry the sacred tent and their own banners.

—Numbers 2:17

The sacred tent, or tabernacle of meeting, was set right in the middle of the whole moving camp of the Israelites. It represented the presence of God Himself with His people.

The camp of the Levites—the group of people God had chosen to serve Him by caring for the tabernacle—surrounded it as they marched. Not only protecting it, but serving as intermediaries between the people and their Lord.

It's a fascinating sight to imagine: hordes of people moving in order, staying with their family groups, marching under their banners. And God at their very heart.

And it's a picture to keep in your mind as you face your wilderness travels today. Moving purposefully forward, meeting whatever obstacles and opportunities come. With God Himself at the very heart of your life.

[The Levi tribe] will work at the sacred tent for him
and for all the Israelites.

—Numbers 3:7

The Levites had their work cut out for them.
God selected them to serve the needs of the high
priest, Aaron, and his sons.

They cared for all the furnishings in the sacred
tent, or tabernacle—a mammoth task made even
more difficult by constant setting up and taking
down on the journey.

And they did all they could to enable the
whole congregation of Israel to worship God in
the tabernacle with as little difficulty as possible.

God wanted to ensure that His people could
commune with Him readily. He wanted everything in place to enable the people to approach
Him freely. Without distractions or frustrations
to hinder their heartfelt worship.

In the wilderness, that took a whole tribe to
accomplish. Now, it's your responsibility to keep
the way clear and the doors open. So you can approach God at any moment in worship and
praise.

The Kohathites will be responsible for carrying the sacred objects used in worship at the sacred tent.

—*Numbers 4:4*

The Kohathites, a branch of the tribe of Levi, were given specific responsibilities regarding the care of the sacred tent, or tabernacle. God outlined them in Numbers 4. They moved the furnishings of the tabernacle, even the most holy things. Aaron and his sons would cover them because they were so holy that if the Kohathites touched them or even saw them, they would die.

It was an honor. Yet it was hard work. And it seemed pretty mundane. To top it off, they could lose their lives performing the task.

There are all kinds of ways we can serve God and our fellow humans. Most of them are hard work and often boring. But if they are not performed, God's will is not accomplished.

God has called and gifted His children—each one of us—to serve in specific ways. What task has He given you? Remember the Kohathites as you fulfill God's calling to serve.

You must confess your guilt and pay the victim in full for whatever damage has been done, plus a fine of twenty percent.

—Numbers 5:7

Confession. Speaking the truth. Acknowledging the wrong. Agreeing with God that His will has been broken. Owning the responsibility. Clearing the conscience.

Restitution. Asking for forgiveness. Making amends. Going above and beyond the call of duty to set right what had been wrong. Starting over anew.

When someone sins, both confession and restitution are necessary to make it right. In monetary terms, the sinner was to pay back what was taken and more—20 percent more. The sin may not involve money or possessions, but the principle is there: Restitution is made by paying back more than what was taken.

Today, take the time for some self-examination. Search your conscience and your heart for ways you may have hurt someone else. Ask God for wisdom to make the situation right again. Then make arrangements to do it in His power.

Say to the people of Israel: If any of you want to dedicate yourself to me by vowing to become a Nazirite. . . .

—Numbers 6:2

Nazirites were Jews who took a special vow of dedication and consecration to God, usually for a certain period of time. In Numbers 6, God outlined how to make the vow and demonstrate it to the people of Israel.

In our day, a very few souls feel called to a special relationship with God. They may not follow the procedure outlined in Numbers, but the heart is the same. They sense a desire to utterly commit themselves to the Lord and His will, devoting themselves to prayer and service—whether for a specified time or as long as they live.

In truth, God would have each of His children so dedicated and consumed by His love. A lifetime may be unrealistic—although it is certainly possible. But could you devote an hour to thinking only of the Lord?

The LORD bless you and keep you; the LORD make His face shine upon you, and be gracious to you; the LORD lift up His countenance upon you, and give you peace.

—Numbers 6:24–26 (NKJV)

In this familiar benediction, God blessed Aaron and his sons through Moses.

Today, hear it as though it is God speaking to you. Feel the abundant grace and glory of it. Accept it as a promise to you.

"The Lord bless you and keep you." To bless is to favor, to demonstrate grace toward. To keep is to protect and maintain as part of the family.

"The Lord make His face shine upon you, and be gracious to you." God's face shines on those He accepts and loves. He pours out His grace—His unmerited favor—on His children.

"The Lord lift up His countenance upon you, and give you peace." God looks on you as a loving father beams over his child. He provides you with the peace—a sense of well-being and rightness—that you need to face the day.

Hear God speaking to you today. And accept His love, care, and grace.

Have someone make two trumpets out of hammered silver. These will be used to call the people together and to give the signal for moving your camp.

—*Numbers 10:2*

God offered a simple solution for directing, managing, and keeping the mammoth group of Israelites in order: Make trumpets, and use them to announce His intentions—to assemble or march or battle or celebrate.

Today, we have alarm clocks, beepers, watch alarms, and other aural signals to direct us. And perhaps we become enslaved to them. To the point that we can't hear God in the midst of them.

In Israel's case, God's Word was given through Moses to the priests to the people. The signals they heard were the direct will of God. The signals we hear often crowd God out.

Today, try an experiment. Try to do without as many of those alarms and signals as you can, just for one day. Listen instead to your inner trumpets. Is God trying to tell you something you haven't been able to hear?

While I am talking with you there, I will give them some of your authority, so they can share responsibility for my people. You will no longer have to care for them by yourself.

—Numbers 11:17

Moses was in the overwhelming position of being the personal counselor, judge, and minister to the entire nation of Israel. And he came to the end of his resources.

Finally, Moses erupted in a burst of self-pity and complaint: "Lord, what have I done to deserve this? How can I possibly answer all their requests? I can't handle it any more."

Moses asked for what he needed. And God answered. He called on Moses to gather seventy of the elders of the land, leaders who could share the burden with him.

Where are you pushing your limits? God can answer your need. If you ask Him.

DAY 161

I can do anything! Watch and you'll see my words
come true.

—Numbers 11:23

Moses was besieged by hundreds of thousands
of hungry, tired, complaining people who demanded meat to eat. Where in the world could
he get provisions sufficient for an unruly crowd
like that?

He was beside himself with anxiety. Filled
with frustration, he turned to the Lord God, saying in effect, "Look, Lord, these are Your people,
and this is Your problem. How in the world are
You going to fix this problem?"

God's response certainly put Moses in his
place: "I can do anything!" God's power hadn't
changed. Moses' faith had.

Doubt may still overwhelm us at times. God
has provided so much in the past, but when the
next need comes up we wonder how He can possibly handle it—since we can't.

Refresh your vision of God and His power and
provision for you today.

I, the LORD, speak to prophets in visions and dreams. But my servant Moses is the leader of my people. He sees me face to face, and everything I say to him is perfectly clear.

—Numbers 12:6–8a

Moses had a unique relationship with God. Even God's prophets—His human messengers to the people—received God's word in a vision or a dream. That was as close as God came even to those holy people.

But Moses' faithfulness and position opened the door all the way between him and God. As a result, God explained that He spoke "face to face," as a friend to a friend.

God and Moses spoke clearly to each other. It was as intimate as a relationship can be.

That kind of relationship with God was unique in Moses' day. But Christ has empowered and enabled us to experience the same close, intimate bond with God.

If we are faithful enough to risk pursuing it.

I have done great things for these people, and they still reject me by refusing to believe in my power.

—Numbers 14:11

How long will you ignore God?

How long will you fail to remember all the wondrous things He's done for you?

How long will it take before you spend time with Him in prayer and meditation as your top priority every day?

How long will you not believe His promises of hope and provision and care?

How long will it be before you obey His call on your life?

How long will you continue to give a good "performance"?

How long before you take a stand for what's right?

How long will it be before you cleanse your life of the influences, the behaviors, the attitudes that drag you down?

How long will you reject Him?

DAY 164

In answer to your prayer, I do forgive them.
—Numbers 14:20

Once again Moses begged God to forgive the people of their sin and selfishness. Once again he put his life on the line for the entire nation. And once again God heard Moses' plea and pardoned the people.

Not that there wouldn't be judgment: Their sinful actions would have serious consequences. But God would not abandon them, utterly destroy them, or break His covenant promise to them.

Once again we see the mysterious power of prayer. We believe in a God who is sovereign and all-knowing. Who knows everything from the beginning to the end. Whose purposes are sure and whose will is unbreakable.

And yet, He is a God who desires our prayers. He wants to know the burdens on our hearts. He wants us to ask for what we need for ourselves or for others. He wants us to fellowship with Him in holy conversation.

And He is a God who listens to our bold, honest prayers. Just as He listened to Moses'.

JUNE 12

But as surely as I live and my power has no limit, I swear that not one of these Israelites will enter the land I promised to give their ancestors. These people have seen my power in Egypt and in the desert, but they will never see Canaan. They have disobeyed and tested me too many times.

—Numbers 14:21–23

God revealed the consequences of the nation's spiritual blindness and rebellion. Because they continually put Him to the test—demanding His deliverance and provision while at the same time doubting both—and because they wouldn't obey Him when they did hear Him, they would not see the Promised Land.

God is a God of forgiveness. But there are still consequences to sin. Consequences that can haunt a person for the rest of his or her life.

You may still be struggling with a consequence of a wrong choice you made years ago. Make peace with the circumstances of your life, and you'll discover new peace in life. With yourself. And with God.

But my servant Caleb isn't like the others. So because he has faith in me, I will allow him to cross into Canaan, and his descendants will settle there.

—Numbers 14:24

Caleb—with Joshua, God's chosen leader of His people after Moses—stood out from the crowd. Against the odds, he stood up for what he knew was right, what he accepted as God's will. Against the power of peer pressure, he tried to rally the nation to go into the Promised Land and claim it. Despite the dangers. Despite the opposition. Despite the fears.

Because he knew the benefits would far outweigh the drawbacks. And because he knew that God was able to give them success.

Unfortunately, Caleb was outvoted. And God's judgment fell on the nation—at least on all of them except Joshua and Caleb.

Why? Because Caleb wasn't "like the others." He had utter faith in God's plan.

We can have such faith, too. It takes knowing God, trusting God, and walking with God—fully. And then living life just as fully.

Your children will wander around in this desert forty years, suffering because of your sins, until all of you are dead.

—Numbers 14:33

How many times had the grumbling Israelites complained that they would rather die in the wilderness than follow Moses? Finally, rebuked by their rebellion, God granted their request.

His judgment was firm. The people would wander in the wilderness for forty more years— one year for each day the spies traveled through the Promised Land.

Most of the spies had feared what they saw: the dangers, the difficulties, the hard work. Two—Joshua and Caleb—saw only the blessings and the opportunities.

What a tragic loss of opportunity, blessing, and freedom! Think about it. And ask yourself, What blessings am I cutting myself off from as a result of my fear, my ignorance, my lack of trust? What is keeping me wandering in this desert of the soul? When will I take possession of abundant life?

You shall have no inheritance in their land, nor shall you have any portion among them; I am your portion and your inheritance among the children of Israel.

—Numbers 18:20 (NKJV)

There was bad news and there was good news for Aaron and the priests of Israel.

The bad news was, they would have no inheritance in the land. No parcel of property. That must have been disappointing.

Ah, but the good news: "I am your portion and your inheritance among the children of Israel." They were actually favored above the other children of Israel. They would have God Himself.

He would provide everything they needed. He would give them a life far richer in significance, blessing, and joy than any plot of land could offer.

What a gift God was giving them!

Even if you don't have any land to call your own, can you see the many blessings God has given you, too?

Moses, get your walking stick. Then you and Aaron call the people together and command that rock to give you water. That's how you will provide water for the people of Israel and their livestock.

—Numbers 20:7–8

The people were thirsty. And they were complaining just as mightily as the previous generation had.

God instructed Moses to take his walking stick and speak to the rock. Then the water would flow.

In his anger and his frustration with the grumbling children of Israel, Moses taunted them, then struck the rock twice. Water gushed out. The need was met.

But not in the way God had proscribed. And that revealed Moses' lack of trust in God's way of provision. As a result, Moses could not enter the land.

A harsh judgment? So it seems. But it shows God's absolute holiness. It reveals that His will must be followed.

Make a snake out of bronze and place it on top of a pole. Anyone who gets bitten can look at the snake and won't die.

—Numbers 21:8

Snakes whose bites burned like fire were inflicted on the rebelliously grumbling people of Israel. God had had enough of their complaining yet again, so they were disciplined. And it worked. Many of the Israelites begged for forgiveness.

So God instructed Moses to fabricate a snake and set it on a pole. Those who had been bitten by the snakes could look up to it and live.

In John's gospel, Jesus said, "And the Son of Man must be lifted up, just as that metal snake was lifted up by Moses in the desert. Then everyone who has faith in the Son of Man will have eternal life" (3:14–15).

God says, the only thing the snake-bitten Israelites had to do was look to the snake on the pole, and they would live. Jesus says, the only thing anyone has to do is look in faith to His work on the cross, and he or she will live eternally. What are you looking at? What are you seeing?

God is no mere human! He doesn't tell lies or change his mind. God always keeps his promises.

—Numbers 23:19

The prophet Balaam brought this word from God to Balak, the king of Moab. And it tells us how trustworthy God's Word is.

We know we sometimes shade the truth, tell white lies, or even lie outright. And we know just about everyone else does, too.

When we say we'll do something for someone, we may or may not. Maybe if we think of it we will. Or maybe not. We may even promise to do something. But being human, we may not keep that promise.

So when God says He will do something because He said He would, we tend to doubt it. He doesn't really mean it, does He? Yes, He does.

God doesn't say anything frivolously. So when you read His Word, you can trust it to be true. And that's the same kind of trust He wants to see exhibited in His children, too.

Instead of punishing them, I forgave them. So because of the loyalty that Phinehas showed, I solemnly promise that he and his descendants will always be my priests.

—Numbers 25:12–13

Phinehas, Aaron's grandson, had zealously taken steps to deal with sin in the camp—sin that had brought about a plague on the land. And as a result, he received God's special blessing. A solemn promise that he and his descendants would live a life of peace in the power and presence of God. A commitment from God to protect and preserve and give purpose forever. What greater gift could God give to His child?

Yet, though Phinehas was singled out, God now deals with all of His children through Jesus in the same way. He promises an abundant life. All we need do is accept it. Take the steps to live it. And then experience it.

Is it for real? Is it a pie-in-the-sky-by-and-by promise that really doesn't affect our daily lives? Why not try it and find out for yourself?

One day you will go up into the Abarim Mountains, and from there you will see the land I am giving the Israelites. After you have seen it, you will die, just like your brother Aaron.

—Numbers 27:12–13

His life had been long and fruitful. He had walked with God more intimately than anyone else had. He had faced tremendous pressures, incredible opposition, seemingly impossible circumstances, and he had seen God shatter them all.

And toward the end of his days, Moses was invited by God to take a sneak preview of the grand and glorious promise that had been held out to him and to Israel for as long as he had lived.

By God's command, he would not accompany the people into the land. Moses would instead be ushered into a far greater and more glorious place: the presence of God Himself. He would commune with his Friend face-to-face forever and ever.

That's the same destiny each child of God can look forward to as well. Let that promise dwell in you today.

DAY 174

Joshua son of Nun can do the job. Place your hands
on him to show that he is the one to take your place.
Then go with him and have him stand in front of
Eleazar the priest and the Israelites. Appoint Joshua
as their new leader.

—Numbers 27:18–19

A new generation of leadership for Israel was
ushered in as God instructed Moses to commis-
sion Joshua before the nation as the new leader.

Joshua had proven himself to be a man of
God. And now the weight of the responsibility of
leadership would fall on his shoulders. But the
Spirit dwelled within him to carry him through
it. And that was the only way he could succeed.

A person filled with the Spirit of the living
God can face tremendous odds, fearful circumstances, overwhelming dangers, and huge responsibilities. And win.

That same Power is available to you today.
The same Spirit dwells within you. He is available to give you the power and wisdom you need.

On the first day of the seventh month, you must rest from your work and come together to celebrate at the sound of the trumpets.

—Numbers 29:1

God called His people to a celebration. A day to stop the routine, make offerings, and prepare the heart for the annual Day of Atonement.

But there's a joy about this day that sets it apart. A day of celebration, music, laughter, joyful noise. A day of gathering together to feast and fellowship and praise the Lord.

A day to set all the fears and pains and burdens aside, and focus on the moment. To heed God's call to come together and celebrate.

A day to blow the trumpets.

Maybe you need that kind of day today. Nothing profound. No deep significance. No heavy responsibilities. Just a day to celebrate.

Make some noise today.

When one of you men makes a promise to the
LORD, you must keep your word.

—Numbers 30:2

Moses reviewed the law of God with the heads
of the twelve tribes of Israel. And he started with
vows.

The words God's people utter in promise to
God are holy. They are important. They are unbreakable.

Yes, there's room for grace. There's opportunity to change. But that shouldn't excuse us from
considering our promises to God to be vital to
keep.

And that commitment should permeate all
our speech. As Jesus put it, "When you make a
promise, say only 'Yes' or 'No'" (Matt. 5:37).

Say what you mean and mean what you say.
Be honest and trustworthy. Live in such a way
that people can count on your doing what you
say you will do.

That doesn't mean you don't have limits and
boundaries. You can still say no. But mean it
when you do say it.

Give the people of Israel this message: When you
cross the Jordan River and enter Canaan, you must
force out the people living there. Destroy their idols
and tear down their altars.

—Numbers 33:51–52

The Israelites were on the brink of a future of
freedom and joy, dwelling with their God in the
land He had promised them. And yet that future
depended on driving out the godless, wicked inhabitants who dwelled in the land.

The Israelites were to remove every idol and
altar. Such things would pollute the atmosphere
if left in their midst. So God commanded them,
as they prepared for new life, to clean up the old.

When we enter new life with God, we may
bring with us a lot of unhealthy behaviors, attitudes, and memories. We can work to remove
them and grow above them. And we should. But
that can only happen effectively in God's
strength.

Tell the people of Israel: After you have crossed the Jordan River and are settled in Canaan, choose Safe Towns, where a person who has accidentally killed someone can run for protection.

—Numbers 35:10–11

God told the Levites to oversee Safe Towns, or cities of refuge. They were places where someone who had accidentally killed another could find safety to avoid being killed by the dead person's family in revenge.

They weren't places to run away from justice; they permitted the offender to be protected while justice was being carried out, while the officials conducted an investigation. Then it could be determined whether the death was caused accidentally or not, and what punishment was prudent.

That God would call for such cities shows His desire for justice. And it tells us that whatever happens in life by God's will is absolutely right. He has our best interests at heart.

I, the LORD, live among you people of Israel, so your
land must be kept pure.

—Numbers 35:33

As the children of Israel moved into the land,
God was moving in to live right with them.

The land was special to God. It was to be holy,
for it was His dwelling place among the people
on the earth. So He commanded His children to
keep it pure. Not to live there in sin. Not to pursue false gods.

God dwells in your midst today, too. He lives
right with you, wherever you are. Your relationship with Him is different from that with the Israelites, for He has literally taken up residence
within you.

Your body is like the land the Israelites inhab-
ited. What you do with your body will affect
your relationship with the God who dwells
within. Nurture it. Care for it. Keep it healthy.

I give you this land, just as I promised your ancestors Abraham, Isaac, and Jacob. Now you must go and take the land.

—Deuteronomy 1:8

After years of slaving in Egypt and years of wandering in the wilderness, the nation of Israel stood at the brink of the Promised Land.

God had set it before them, and He commanded them to go in and take it.

After all, it had been promised to their forefathers. And though their lack of faith kept them from it forty years earlier, they were ready.

They really had no idea what challenges awaited them, but they had a good idea. And they trusted God enough to take Him at His word. To go in and possess the land.

Perhaps God has called you to a "land." A ministry, a service, a calling. Something you're not sure you can handle. Will you put Him off? Or will you—in His power—go in and take what He has set before you?

The LORD our God will lead the way. He will fight on our side, just as he did when we saw him do all those things to the Egyptians. And you know that the LORD has taken care of us the whole time we've been in the desert, just as you might carry one of your children.

—Deuteronomy 1:30–31

Before the nation of Israel entered the land, Moses reviewed their history with the people. And his words were both challenging and comforting, rebuking and redemptive.

The Lord God would go before them into the land, Moses explained, preparing the way, clearing the path. And as they went, He would fight for them—just as He did in Egypt. He would carry them along—just as He did in the wilderness, all the way up to the present moment.

In the same way, God carries each of us as we might carry a child. And when we realize that and keep it in our minds, our whole perspective changes. We see the promise fulfilled rather than the difficult path ahead.

The LORD has helped us and taken care of us during the past forty years that we have been in this huge desert. We've had everything we needed, and the LORD has blessed us and made us successful in whatever we have done.

—Deuteronomy 2:7

It may not have seemed much like a blessing.

The nation of Israel had wandered in the desert for forty years. The people needed food, water, and clothing. They couldn't understand why their problems kept compounding themselves. They lived from a negative perspective, seeing what was wrong in every situation. Rather than seeing the hand of God at work in their lives.

All along the way, He was blessing them. Protecting them. Preparing them. Parenting them. But they couldn't see it.

What if they had followed the Lord in trust and faith? How might the story have been different?

You may identify with the nation of Israel. And you realize you want to open your eyes and your heart to what God is doing on your behalf. You can do that today if you choose to.

Today I will start making all other nations afraid of you. They will tremble with fear when anyone mentions you, and they will be terrified when you show up.

—Deuteronomy 2:25

The little band of Israelites was going to cause a stir in the world.

Of all the nations of the area, they certainly weren't the strongest, best armed, or best trained group of people. And yet, God told them their enemies would hear reports of their strength and fear them.

When God's power is at work, free and unfettered by our doubt or fear, it makes an impact on the world around us. But our goal is not to make others cower; it is to draw them into God's presence. That's why God's love is so important.

Open yourself today as a channel not only for God's power but also for His love and grace. And the impact you make on those around you will never be forgotten.

He is your God. I am telling you everything he has commanded, so don't add anything or take anything away.

—Deuteronomy 4:2

When God gave His Word to the people, it wasn't a series of options. It was His Word. It was given for their total benefit. It was complete in everything. It was life.

So God gave them this warning not to add to it or subtract from it. It's a total package. And fully obeyed, it would bring life and peace and joy.

But humankind can't seem to leave well enough alone. The Israelites eventually built a complicated structure of additional rules, regulations, and explanations that would collapse upon itself. And they would ignore whole sections of God's Word, glossing over parts, conveniently forgetting others, and explaining away still others.

In our heart of hearts, we do the same thing. We reinterpret His Word to let ourselves off the hook. Or we just ignore it and hope it goes away.

Today, renew your appreciation for the full Word of God.

DAY 185

Only take heed to yourself, and diligently keep yourself, lest you forget the things your eyes have seen, and lest they depart from your heart all the days of your life. And teach them to your children and your grandchildren.

—Deuteronomy 4:9 (NKJV)

It starts with each individual and spreads out from there.

God says, "Take heed to yourself." Mind your own heart first. Keep His Word living and active in your mind and your life. Live by His will. Develop those behaviors as a lifestyle. Work on your own issues. Keep on your own path with God. Then—and only then—teach the truth to your children and grandchildren.

Out of a life of wisdom and serenity with God can come great insight for others. But teaching and advising others without that solid foundation can lead only to problems and frustrations.

As parent or friend, you should offer your support and encouragement as best you can. But first you should continually strive to become ever healthier, stronger, and devoted to God.

"Take heed." What areas of your life need your attention—and God's loving hand?

DAY 186

Bring the people of Israel here. I want to speak to them so they will obey me as long as they live, and so they will teach their children to obey me too.

—Deuteronomy 4:10

When God gave the nation of Israel His word, He set into motion a process that should still mark our lives today.

"Bring the people of Israel here." There is strength in coming together in fellowship.

"I want to speak to them." This is the foundational activity for God's people. Hearing and understanding His Word.

"So they will obey me." We are part of a larger group, but we must focus on our own relationship with God, learning to obey Him and walk with Him in trust.

"So they will teach their children to obey me too." Out of a full heart is the overflow of wisdom, love, and peace. When our relationship with God is living and active and strong, we can teach others His way—both by our words and by our very lives.

Do you see the progression? To gather, to hear, to obey, to teach others. It is a way of life that builds strength and purpose, peace and joy.

The LORD will be angry if you worship other gods, and he can be like a fire destroying everything in its path.

—Deuteronomy 4:24

We have a mate. We have our children. We have a best friend. We have a number of friends. We have our neighbors. We have our work. We have our play. We have our personal growth.

And—oh, yes—we have God.

But that kind of attitude won't work with God. He's not just one of the many influences in our lives. He demands preeminence. And He is worthy of it.

Finding fulfillment on the basis of our relationships is like building a house on shifting sand. But building a life on the foundation of a solid relationship with God creates a healthy, growing, living environment in which all our other relationships and responsibilities can flow.

God is jealous for our total dedication and attention. And we will only benefit if we give both to Him.

Remember that the LORD is the only true God, whether in the sky above or on the earth below.

—Deuteronomy 4:39

Here's the starting point in life. Knowing as a matter of absolute, unshakable fact that the God you worship is the God of all the universe.

No other way will work. There is no other god to help. There is no other source of power to succeed. Not even within yourself.

Remember this: It's God or nothing.

We can work and work, striving to grow on our own, trying to build the power we need to be healthy, strong individuals, working to serve and support others in appropriate ways. And ultimately, we will get nowhere.

But seek to do all that in the power of God, under the guidance of His Spirit, and miracles can happen. Just remember the starting point. And keep moving from there.

The LORD our God made an agreement with our nation at Mount Sinai. That agreement wasn't only with our ancestors but with us, who are here today.
—*Deuteronomy 5:2–3*

Forty years earlier, God had made an agreement, or a covenant, with the nation of Israel. But they broke it. And as a result, God prohibited them from entering the land. He waited until that generation had died out. And a new generation was poised to enter the land.

Moses explained that, in truth, the agreement was made with this new generation at Mount Sinai—even though they hadn't been born yet.

Still, God kept the agreement. And because this generation would experience its benefits, they were in effect the original recipients of it.

When God says something, its effects are eternal. Just because He spoke to the Israelites, the prophets, the apostles, and others doesn't mean He wasn't speaking to us, too.

God's Word is sure, His promises unbreakable. Strengthen your trust in them today. Read them. Apply them. Live them. Appreciate them.

I wish they would always worship me with fear and trembling and be this willing to obey me! Then they and their children would always enjoy a successful life.

—Deuteronomy 5:29

God eloquently expressed His deepest desire for His people.

He created them with the power of choice. He didn't create robots or puppets on a string. He made individuals with wills. He made His desires known for them, but He left the decision as to whether to hear it or not up to them.

So He wished their hearts were strong enough to trust Him and revere Him. He wished their wills were strong enough to obey Him. Not for His sake, but for their own.

This is still God's desire for His people. And still His promise.

But our stubbornness can be our downfall. Our yearning to be independent and strong can ultimately cost us. If only we would surrender to God's will and be strong in Him. Imagine the delight in His heart. And in our hearts.

Follow [the LORD's commands], because they make a path that will lead to a long successful life in the land the LORD your God is giving you.

—*Deuteronomy 5:33*

God's blessing.

We all want it. But when we read a verse like this, it seems that we have to earn it. Do something to get it. It feels like a business transaction rather than the experience of God's abundant grace.

Of course, the Israelites lived under circumstances different than ours. They lived under the law. And the law—as the apostle Paul explains in the New Testament—was given to show us just how miserably sinful we are on our own.

Jesus Christ gave us the better way. Acceptance by God because we are clothed with His own righteousness.

God says, "If you pursue My will, the natural consequence will be a life that's free and powerful and peaceful and rewarding."

Obedience in following the Lord's commands opens the door to true fulfillment. God invites you to walk right in.

Hear, O Israel: The LORD our God, the LORD is one! You shall love the LORD your God with all your heart, with all your soul, and with all your strength.
—*Deuteronomy 6:4–5 (NKJV)*

This was a special passage to the Jews. They repeated it daily, calling it the *Shema* for the first word in it: "Hear."

They considered it a summary of their faith, the fundamental truth of their religion. But it looks forward to the fuller truth we know in Christ. The word for God is plural. So "the LORD our God [plural], the LORD is one!" points to the doctrine of the Trinity—God the Father, Son, and Holy Spirit.

The Shema starts with this God who loves us and commands us to love Him with every fiber of our being—heart, soul, strength.

Obedience to God is to arise out of a strong sense of love and devotion to Him. And the love that generates our obedience requires full concentration, total commitment, and the involvement of our minds, our souls, our wills, our bodies.

Memorize his laws and tell them to your children over and over again. Talk about them all the time, whether you're at home or walking along the road or going to bed at night, or getting up in the morning.

—Deuteronomy 6:6–7

God's Word is to saturate the lives of His children.

Moses proclaimed to the Israelites that God's commands should be treasured in their hearts. That is the source from which everything we say and do arises. And as we keep His truth in our hearts and minds, our actions and attitudes will reflect His will.

But God's Word isn't to stay there in the heart. It's to be taught diligently to others—particularly children—wherever we may be. God's truth should be with you at all times.

A life saturated by God's Word has peace, joy, purpose, hope. And when the Spirit of God is set loose to work out the Word of God within you, that is a life worth living.

Write down copies and tie them to your wrists and foreheads to help you obey them. Write these laws on the door frames of your homes and on your town gates.

—Deuteronomy 6:8–9

Moses encouraged the Israelites to keep God's words ever before them.

Even to tying them to their wrists, so that in working they would always be reminded of God's will. Even to placing them on their foreheads, to remind themselves and one another of the guiding force of His words on their minds. Even to writing them on the door frames, so that in their coming and going, God's truth would refresh their minds and keep them focused.

Many Jews took the admonitions seriously and literally, wearing phylacteries—little boxes containing summaries of the law—on the forehead and left arm, and attaching them to their homes.

God is calling His children to make His truth part of every aspect of our lives. At home, work or play, every word, every deed, should reflect His love and care.

Israel, you are the chosen people of the LORD your
God. There are many nations on this earth, but he
chose only Israel to be his very own.

—Deuteronomy 7:6

God's people are unique. They were specially
chosen by the God of the universe to be the
channel of His blessing to the world at large.

They were therefore holy. Set apart for His
purposes and pleasure. Above all others, not in
terms of equality, but in terms of their unique relationship with God.

They were a people chosen by God for Himself. We don't know why He chose Abraham or
worked so diligently with the Israelites.

But God treasured them. He loved them. He
delighted in them. And He still does.

Through the Israelites came the Savior of the
world, Jesus Christ. And through Him, we are
grafted in to the chosen people. So we are God's
people today. We who follow Christ, who have
been bought by His blood.

You were the weakest of all nations, but the LORD chose you because he loves you and because he had made a promise to your ancestors. Then with his mighty arm, he rescued you from the king of Egypt, who had made you his slaves.

—Deuteronomy 7:7–8

Why did God love the Israelites? Why did He choose them from among all others to bless and use and care for? Moses explained that it wasn't because they were better than all the others. They weren't bigger, stronger, or smarter. In fact, "you were the weakest of all nations."

Apparently, the Lord loves a challenge. But that's a trait consistent through the Scriptures. He uses the weak to show His strength (see 2 Cor. 12:10).

God loved and chose the Israelites just as He loved and chose us: despite ourselves. Jesus said, "My kindness is all you need. My power is strongest when you are weak" (2 Cor. 12:9).

The LORD will love you and bless you by giving you many children and plenty of food, wine, and olive oil. Your herds of cattle will have many calves, and your flocks of sheep will have many lambs.

—Deuteronomy 7:13

What happens when you follow God with a whole heart?

Moses offers the answer. God will love you, bless you, prosper you. Your children, the work of your hands, your provisions, your property, will also be blessed.

Does that mean you earn God's favor? No. Nothing you could do could cause you to be perfectly acceptable in God's eyes. Unfortunately, the Israelites would ultimately prove that to be so. Their disobedience would cause God to send them off to exile in discipline for their wickedness.

Now you come to God through the perfect work of His Son. It all comes through Christ. Of course, God wants you to be obedient and faithful. To move in God's will—forward, outward, and upward. Make that your life goal.

You may be thinking, "How can we destroy these nations? They are more powerful than we are." But stop worrying! Just remember what the LORD your God did to Egypt and its king.

—Deuteronomy 7:17–18

When you face a major challenge, think of the Israelites.

They were preparing to enter a land that wasn't theirs. And they were supposed to go in, defeat and destroy the inhabitants, clean out all their influences, and settle in. And a lot of those inhabitants were big and mean and strong.

How would you feel? Like the Israelites, probably afraid. Even terrified. But Moses said to them, why be afraid? Just remember what the Lord God did in Egypt to enable the Israelites to leave bondage there.

God can do anything. So what "enemies" are you facing today? What big unfinished task or confrontation or major step forward awaits you? "You shall not be terrified of them; for the LORD your God, the great and awesome God, is among you" (v. 21 NKJV).

So He made you go hungry. Then he gave you manna, a kind of food that you and your ancestors had never even heard about. The LORD was teaching you that people need more than food to live—they need every word that the LORD has spoken.

—Deuteronomy 8:3

Why did the Israelites wander in the wilderness for forty years before being allowed to enter in? Moses answered: "Don't forget how the LORD your God has led you through the desert for the past forty years. He wanted to find out if you were truly willing to obey him and depend on him" (v. 2).

God told the people to obey, but He didn't tell them how they would be able to obey. All they could do was trust Him. So when they realized they had no food, all they could do was wait for Him. And He provided manna for their bodies. And His Word for their souls.

We need physical sustenance. But just as important is spiritual nourishment, enabling us to live fully in the will of God. God has provided everything you need for your journey. Feed on it.

You aren't good—you are stubborn! No, the LORD is going to help you, because the nations that live there are evil, and because he wants to keep the promise he made to your ancestors Abraham, Isaac, and Jacob.

—Deuteronomy 9:5–6

God explained that the reason He had given the Israelites the land, and would give them the power and ability to possess it, wasn't that they had earned it. It wasn't a reward for their righteousness. After all, He said they were stubborn.

Rather, He was giving them victory because He was so displeased with the wickedness of the nations dwelling there that He was determined to drive them out. And because He had sworn to give the land to Abraham, Isaac, and Jacob, and He was determined to keep His word.

The same is true with us. Nothing we have done could earn the favor we experience from God's hand. It is only through God's grace, His unmerited favor, that we can enjoy our relationship with Him through Christ.

DAY 201

People of Israel, what does the LORD your God want from you? The LORD wants you to respect and follow him, to love and serve him with all your heart and soul, and to obey his laws and teachings that I am giving you today. Do this, and all will go well for you.

—Deuteronomy 10:12–13

Life 101, according to God. Here's the syllabus:

Respect the Lord. Know who He is. Realize His awesome power and authority in your life.

Follow Him. Read His Word; understand it; live it.

Love Him. Love Him from a heart of dedication and devotion.

Serve Him with all your heart and soul. Make your life a ministry of praise for Him, an outreach by word and deed to those in need. Wholeheartedly.

Obey His teachings. Follow His Word and His will throughout your life.

That's what God requires. That's His desire for each child.

You have a choice—do you want the LORD to bless you, or do you want him to put a curse on you? Today I am giving you his laws, and if you obey him, he will bless you. But if you disobey him and worship those gods that have never done anything for you, the LORD will put a curse on you.

—*Deuteronomy 11:26–28*

The choice was set before the Israelites. It was blessing or cursing. It was life or death.

We can argue that life isn't so black and white. There is so much to consider before making such decisions. We prefer to analyze the details first. To weigh all the benefits to see if we'll come out ahead.

God is making it as clear as He possibly can for our own good. And boiled down to the basics, there are two kinds of life: obedience and disobedience; blessing and cursing; strength and weakness; fulfillment and disillusionment.

You've already made your decision. What is it?

If the prophet says this, don't listen! The LORD your God will be watching to find out whether or not you love him with all your heart and soul.

—Deuteronomy 13:3

Sometimes a teacher or preacher will come on the scene with some exciting new ways of teaching, revealing some fascinating truths about God and life we may never have considered. And without a spirit of discernment, we may accept what the person says before realizing he or she is not talking about the same god we are.

In Israel's culture, that was a frequent scenario. So Moses warned the people to test a prophet or a dreamer.

God wanted the Israelites to be so in love with Him, so dedicated to living their lives with Him, that they would immediately know the truth of what they heard. And reject whatever was false.

His desire for you is the same. And in a world overrun with false prophets and unbiblical teachings, it's never been more important to be discerning.

There will always be some Israelites who are poor and needy. That's why I am commanding you to be generous with them.

—Deuteronomy 15:11

Poverty is a fact of life. There will always be some circumstances that cause people to lose their money and their belongings and live in utter need: financial reversals, the death of the breadwinner, poor health, lack of support.

We can work and provide and pay taxes, but there will always be people who need financial help.

Why don't they just get a job? Why don't they do something for themselves? Some can't. Others won't. That's not for us to answer.

The fact is, people in need will always be with us. And God tells us His will regarding them: We are to be generous.

Are you fulfilling that desire of God's heart? Ask God how you can help in your community.

If any of you buy Israelites as slaves, you must set them free after six years. And don't just tell them they are free to leave—give them sheep and goats and a good supply of grain and wine.

—Deuteronomy 15:12–14

As inhumane as slavery can be, the Israelites were given some humane guidelines to follow.

Servanthood didn't have the cultural baggage then that it does now. The excesses and cruelty inflicted in past centuries on persons in forced servitude—even in America—have made the concept unacceptable.

To the Israelites, however, voluntary servitude was an acceptable profession. It offered food, clothing, shelter, a family environment, good hard work, and freedom after six years. Such servants were protected by God from the excesses.

God calls us to servanthood under His loving authority. The greatest leader is the servant of all, Jesus said. How could you be an effective, strong, willing servant of God today?

The bigger the harvest the LORD gives you, the bigger your gift should be.

—Deuteronomy 16:17

We read of the tithe and all the offerings, and we discover that in the Old Testament, God called on His people to give over 30 percent of their income or possessions to the work of the Lord. And we probably don't give anywhere near that to our churches.

Of course, much of that 30 percent helped cover what our taxes do now—support the rulers, protect the nation, and provide needed services—as well as support the temple and priests. But that shouldn't excuse us from being obedient to give as we can to the Lord.

God through Moses gives this basic guideline for giving. As God blesses us with income, we are to give as much as we can to support our churches and other Christian organizations as He leads us.

Today, realize how much—or how little—of your income is available to God. Understand that it is all in His hands. Make specific plans to give as God leads you. And watch how God works.

If the LORD says something will happen, it will happen. And if it doesn't, you will know that the prophet was falsely claiming to speak for the LORD. Don't be afraid of any prophet whose message doesn't come from the LORD.

—Deuteronomy 18:22

Prophets were people, too. Some of them God called to be a channel of His word to His people and to the whole world. Others assumed the mantle of the prophet on their own.

But God gave a very simple test to determine whether what they said really was what He meant. The test was, if their "prophetic word" didn't happen, God did not speak that word. So there was no reason to fear that prophet or to pay attention to him.

God has given us the Bible to guide our lives. And He has given us the Spirit to dwell within us to give us understanding and illumination, the power to carry out His will in our lives, and the discernment to hear His voice clearly. Trust His Word.

Before you are convicted of a crime, at least two witnesses must be able to testify that you did it.

—*Deuteronomy 19:15*

Justice never comes at the hands of one person. Otherwise, anyone with a grudge or some ulterior motive could destroy another person with an accusation with no basis in fact.

Moses declared God's will that any charge against another person must be established by at least two witnesses in order to protect against injustice.

And that's a good reminder to consider if you hear a troubling report from the mouth of one individual about someone you know. Check it out. Were there any other witnesses? Where did the person telling you get the information? Can you ask the person charged what the story is?

Justice is called for. Honesty, fairness, and grace are always in order.

Are those traits marking your life today?

Then you and your family must celebrate by eating a meal at the place of worship to thank the LORD your God for giving you such a good harvest. And remember to invite the Levites and the foreigners who live in your town.

—Deuteronomy 26:11

In joy and appreciation, the Israelites were to offer to God the firstfruits of their land as a token of their thanks to the One who provided everything they needed.

Rejoicing was an essential element of life in God for the Israelites. They had ample opportunity to come to God in thanksgiving for all He had given them.

If we can keep our eyes open for them, life is filled with opportunities for joy. The restorative comradeship of a friend. The loving embrace of a spouse. The frivolous fun of a child at play. The beauty of nature in all its complexity. A step forward in personal growth. A job well done. Each one an opportunity to thank God in joy.

DAY 210

Today I am giving you the laws and teachings of the
LORD your God. Always obey them, and the LORD
will make Israel the most famous and important nation on earth.

—Deuteronomy 28:1–2

God had big plans for Israel. The Israelites
were His crowning achievement among the people of all nations. Through those people, He
would ultimately bless the entire world with His
Son, Jesus Christ. In fact, if the people were obedient to Him and followed His will, He would
make Israel the most famous nation. Unfortunately, their part in that plan was short-circuited
through their selfishness and rebellion.

And that raises some questions to consider
today: What would God do with you if He had
your full attention? What heights could you
reach if you pursued Him in willing trust and
followed Him in joyful obedience?

With His Spirit, imagine where you could be
if you were fully surrendered to Him and His
purposes for you.

The LORD our God hasn't explained the present or the future, but he has commanded us to obey the laws he gave to us and our descendants.

—Deuteronomy 29:29

There are things about life, about the future, about ourselves, that we cannot know. There are other things we can know very clearly and act on. As humans, we tend to focus on the former and let the latter slide.

Moses encouraged the Israelites to leave the unexplained things to God. That's His business. He knows them completely. He has them totally under His loving control. Instead, focus on what He *has* given us: His words. His will. His way of life.

If you are plagued by questions, doubts, and frustrations about the future, if you continually play the what-if game, if you fear the outcome of your life, your focus is in the wrong place.

Start with what you know. Who you are in God. What He has given you to do today. What step you can take today in your personal growth.

You know God's laws, and it isn't impossible to obey them.

—Deuteronomy 30:11

Like the Israelites, we tend to make things a lot harder than they really are.

We look far off to the horizon to discern the will of God for our lives. We feel we need a mystical encounter to fully understand His call on our lives. We think that we need to journey far, and that all our answers will be at the end of that journey.

Moses told the Israelites, not so: God's "commands aren't in heaven, so you can't excuse yourselves by saying, 'How can we obey the LORD's commands? They are in heaven, and no one can go up to get them, then bring them down and explain them to us' " (v. 12).

It is not the big mystery we make it out to be. It is not the unreachable truth we imagine it to be. No. It's right here with you. It is in the Bible.

The question remains: Will you obey it?

I call the sky and the earth to be witnesses that I am offering you this choice. Will you choose for the LORD to make you prosperous and give you a long life? Or will he put you under a curse and kill you? Choose life!

—*Deuteronomy 30:19*

It's a simple choice. Life or death. Prosperity or curse. God's way or our way. But we make it so complicated.

Yes, there are a multitude of decisions and truths to sort through. But all those are intended to be confronted and dealt with after we make the profoundly simple decision about the very foundation of our lives.

Will it be life or death? Will you live pursuing God or your own lusts? Will you move in the flow of His life-giving Spirit or be trapped in the endless eddies of selfishness, rebellion, and depravity? Will you live a life of God-given blessing or wallow in the curses of unfulfillment? Choose life! And live.

Be brave and strong! Don't be afraid of the nations on the other side of the Jordan. The LORD your God will always be at your side, and he will never abandon you.

—Deuteronomy 31:6

B e brave and strong!" Those are the words of God with which Moses encouraged Joshua. The same words God would use to encourage future leaders of Israel.

They were words that Joshua had to hang his hat on. Because without God's trustworthy encouragement, the task he faced would be overwhelming.

We may often tell a child or a friend, "Don't be afraid. It will be okay. I'm here with you." And those can be comforting and reassuring words. The truth, however, is that we really can't do anything about the situation causing the fear. We don't have the power to protect fully.

But when God says those words, you can rest in them. You can let go of the fear and look straight into the situation you face in power and confidence. Not in yourself, but in God.

DAY 215

Everyone must come—men, women, children, and even the foreigners who live in your towns. And each new generation will listen and learn to worship the LORD their God with fear and trembling and to do exactly what is said in God's Law.

—Deuteronomy 31:12–13

Moses wrote down the Law that God had given him, then gave it to the priests—those who were responsible for the spiritual life of the children of God.

Every seven years, Moses instructed them, they were to call the people together and read the Law to them during the Feast of Tabernacles. Everyone was to come and hear. Men, women, children, and even the aliens in the land who were not Israelites. It was that important. Otherwise, how would they know?

Today we have the complete word of God in our Bible. We therefore have the benefit of much greater knowledge of God and His will for us. It is available to all. Are we taking advantage of the opportunity? Are we searching the Scriptures and reflecting on them?

AUGUST 2

DAY 216

Moses, you will soon die. But Israel is going into a land where other gods are worshiped, and Israel will reject me and start worshiping these gods. The people will break the agreement I made with them.

—Deuteronomy 31:16

In the last days of his life, Moses heard this disheartening word from God.

And you have to wonder if Moses thought, *Why have I spent my life leading these people? Is it all for nothing?*

That would be a natural response. The truth is, however, that God through Moses had set into motion a series of events that would culminate in the coming of His Son to earth for the salvation of the whole world.

If Moses had not been obedient, it may never have happened. He trusted that God knew exactly what He was doing, and that the events were all part of a big picture, a big picture that would bring Him ultimate glory.

How would you have responded?

AUGUST 3

I am going to give you the words to a new song. Write them down and teach the song to the Israelites. If they learn it, they will know what I want them to do, and so they will have no excuse for not obeying me.

—Deuteronomy 31:19

God laid out the future of the nation of Israel for Moses. And it was not a pretty picture. The people would rebel against Him and face utter turmoil as a result.

And to keep that eventuality on the minds of the people, to serve as a witness for God in their minds, God gave Moses a song.

It was to be sung by the people. So that when the disasters and difficulties arose as a result of their unfaithfulness, the song would detail exactly what was happening.

Of course, teaching the song could help the people avert the coming crisis. If they would only listen and heed its message. And the message is clear: the coming calamity wouldn't be God's doing, but the natural consequence of their rebellion.

What song would God have you sing? What is its message to you today?

Join with me in praising the wonderful name of the
LORD our God. The LORD is a mighty rock, and he
never does wrong. God can always be trusted to
bring justice.

—Deuteronomy 32:3–4

Moses began his song to the people of Israel.
And he started at the beginning: the foundation
of all truth. It is the Lord.

Today, let Moses' words launch you into a
time of adoration and praise for your loving,
powerful God. The Source of your life. The Protector of your spirit. The Comforter of your soul.
Your Deliverer, Sustainer, Nurturer, Redeemer.

Ascribe greatness to Him. Think of all the
ways He is boundless in power and wisdom and
grace. He is the Rock, strong, mighty, and un-
moving. Everything He does is perfect. He is
right and just in all He does. In Him is all truth.

Let your heart, soul, mind, and spirit praise
Him. Think of His attributes. Recall His great
acts on your behalf. Remind yourself of His wonderful blessings.

DAY 219

But you lie and cheat and are unfaithful to him. You have disgraced yourselves and are no longer worthy to be his children. Israel, the LORD is your Father, the one who created you, but you repaid him by being foolish.

—Deuteronomy 32:5–6

In the light of the glorious truth of God, the people of Israel stood in the shadow. As Moses continued his song, he pointed to a nation who would have disowned their own Father. Who flaunted their self-willed, stubborn hearts, who foolishly rejected His will and His way.

Imagine the broken heart of God, the pain caused by His wayward children. He had created them, delivered them, provided them with a land of milk and honey. But their will was weak. Their heart was divided. And their fate was clear.

We can wonder how they could possibly reject a God who had acted so miraculously and powerfully on their behalf, who had provided their every need. And then we can ask ourselves how far off we are from their example.

Think about past generations. Ask your parents or
any of your elders. They will tell you . . .

—Deuteronomy 32:7

Israel certainly had a history to draw on. Think
back over the first five books of the Bible. Remember what the people had been through, the
blessings of God from generation to generation.

Think of the strength and hope they could de-
rive from those past events. Think of the trust
that could grow in their hearts for God. But the
new generation of Israelites, about to enter the
land, would forget much of the past. They could
learn from their elders, and their faith could
grow. But they would not.

Is there an older person in your church or
community you could learn from? Next opportunity, strike up a conversation. Keep an open
mind. Listen for the ways God has worked in his
or her life. Draw strength from what you hear.
See if you can gain insight into any situation
you're now facing.

The LORD was like an eagle teaching its young to fly, always ready to swoop down and catch them on its back. Israel, the LORD led you, and without the aid of a foreign god.

—Deuteronomy 32:11–12

Moses proclaimed God's gentle, yet purposeful, guiding of the nation of Israel, taking them from a barren desert land and leading them to the new land, their own possession.

And the image used to communicate God's guidance is of a strong eagle that stirs up its nest, rousing the young birds out of the safe confines of their birthplace, pushing them out, then carrying them up on the winds. The eagle hovers protectively over its young as they fly, spreading out its wings to guide, protect, and keep them aloft.

That's how God led the nation. He stirred them up and made them fly with Him.

He has done the same for you. Where would you be today if you had not met God in your desert?

Don't you understand? I am the only God; there are no others. I am the one who takes life and gives it again. I punished you with suffering. But now I will heal you, and nothing can stop me!

—*Deuteronomy 32:39*

As earnestly as the nation would pursue other gods, one basic truth would confront the people time and time again: God is God alone. Their search for truth and power apart from Him would always be fruitless and pointless.

He is the Lord. All life is in His hands. He is the sovereign Ruler over all.

We can know God and trust Him. And we can also take assurance in the fact that those who are in His hands can never be removed. And being in His hands—no matter what happens—we can trust that all is well and will be well.

Even the suffering has a purpose. It brings grief at times. But the healing will come from God's hand as well. It is all in His hands, His strong, capable, gentle hands.

DAY 223

The LORD loves the tribes of Israel, and he protects his people. They listen to his words and worship at his feet.

—Deuteronomy 33:3

Just before his death, Moses called together the people of Israel and offered a blessing on each tribe. He acknowledged that the God of Israel loved His people. God protected them.

The people sat down at His feet, waiting to receive His word, as children before a wise teacher.

That's a picture of your relationship with God as well. He loves you. He protects you. You commune with Him, sit before Him, and listen to His word for you.

It is a peaceful picture. It offers protection and strength and purpose for life.

Bring that picture to mind today. See yourself resting on a lush hillside, gathered together with fellow saints, listening to the loving words of the One who protects you. Let that picture in your mind become reality in your heart as you spend time with Him in prayer.

The LORD has rescued you and given you more blessings than any other nation. He protects you like a shield and is your majestic sword. Your enemies will bow in fear, and you will trample on their backs.

—Deuteronomy 33:29

The last words of Moses. They formed a blessing on Israel—a unique nation. The only nation so specially favored by the Lord of the universe, the one true God. The Israelites alone were rescued by the Lord. They alone enjoyed His shield of protection and help, His sword of majesty and glory. And because they were so favored, their enemies would one day submit to them.

When the Messiah came through the nation Israel, He opened the way for the entire world and all peoples to come directly to God. The blessing has been given; the stage is set for its fulfillment.

And these words can be fulfilled in your life today. As a child of God, a spiritual Israelite, you can know that God is working on your behalf.

Be strong and brave! Be careful to do everything my servant Moses taught you.

—Joshua 1:7

God gave Joshua the encouragement he needed at the beginning of his role as the new leader of Israel. Hundreds of thousands of Israelites stood poised to enter the land and overtake it. The task would require incredible organization, strategic battle skills, and personal strength to pull it all off. But with God, anything was possible.

But the encouragement wasn't to be strong and brave to fulfill the task at hand. Rather, the strength and courage were needed to obey God's word.

That's where our priorities can get confused. We can launch out into doing what we think we should be doing without laying the foundation of a strong, obedient relationship with God.

Joshua set his priorities straight. The job would naturally be fulfilled under his leadership if he focused on hearing and heeding the Lord first. That principle holds true today. Ask yourself if it's a principle you're following.

Never stop reading *The Book of the Law* he gave you. Day and night you must think about what it says. If you obey it completely, you and Israel will be able to take this land.

—Joshua 1:8

God's Law was already in written form. It was available to read and study. And God instructed Joshua to make it part of his daily life. To keep it on his heart, to make it part of his thought life continually.

And not only to read and meditate on it, but to obey it. Knowledge of and obedience to God's Word would make his life work. Success was possible only when pursued in the will of God.

You've made a commitment to yourself to make God's Word part of your life. It opens the door to understanding yourself, your God, and your world better. Keep reading it. Keep meditating on it. Keep making it the engine that drives your life. Then you will have a success the world knows nothing about.

Make yourselves acceptable to worship the LORD, because he is going to do some amazing things for us.
—Joshua 3:5

Israel was preparing to cross the Jordan. It
would be a huge undertaking, an overwhelming
achievement. But an important step had to be
taken first: They had to make themselves "acceptable to worship the Lord." Get their hearts
right with God. Focus on the task and more so
on the One who would provide every need to accomplish it. Take time to draw the strength they
needed from within and from above.

The Israelites didn't know exactly how they'd
get all their people and animals and belongings
across the river. They just knew they would do it
in the Lord's strength, under His direction. And
they knew it was the end of a long journey. The
fulfillment of a great promise.

In our world, we give ourselves little time to
prepare ourselves for something momentous—
physically, emotionally, spiritually. But the best
things take time. Time with God. Give yourself
all the time you need today to prepare your
heart, mind, spirit, and soul to face the next day.

Then you can tell them how the water stopped flowing when the chest was being carried across the river. These rocks will always remind our people of what happened here today.

—Joshua 4:7

The waters of the Jordan were high. The crossing seemed treacherous. But God sent the priests ahead, carrying the chest (the ark of the covenant). And the water stopped flowing. As soon as their feet touched the water, the water retreated. The people crossed over on dry ground.

It was yet another miracle from the hand of God for His people. And to commemorate it, God called each of the twelve tribes to bring a rock for a monument, a memorial for generations to come.

Do you have any "memorial rock" to point back to times when God supernaturally provided for you, cared for you, loved you? Consider an act of God in your life you'd like to remember for years to come. How could you establish a memorial to keep it in your mind?

Then the priests will blast on their trumpets, and everyone else will shout. The wall will fall down, and your soldiers can go straight in from every side.

—Joshua 6:5

Jericho. The first major obstacle to the Israelites' possessing the land. God carefully orchestrated the nation's strategy, and Joshua carried it out. Instructions were explicit. The stage was set.

For seven days the people would march around the walled city. Finally, at the appointed moment, a long blast would signal the marchers to shout as loudly as they could. And the wall would fall.

It would happen precisely as God had outlined. And certainly, it would give the nation confidence to continue its domination of the Promised Land.

Maybe you have experienced little Jerichos— major obstacles to moving ahead dealt with in God's power. Thank Him for those Jerichos.

Our LORD, did you bring us across the Jordan River just so the Amorites could destroy us? This wouldn't have happened if we had agreed to stay on the other side of the Jordan.

—Joshua 7:7

Achan's sin had devastating effects on the entire nation. Achan had absconded with some forbidden booty. And to get the Israelites' attention, God allowed them to experience a major defeat against Ai.

Joshua was distraught. He didn't understand why they had been defeated. God had promised them victory and dominion in the land. What had happened? He demanded to know.

Of course, God put Joshua in his place. But He wasn't frustrated and angry over Joshua's outburst. Certainly, He prized Joshua's honesty and clarity.

Feel free to talk openly and honestly with God. He welcomes it. He may set you straight, but there's no sense harboring hurt or fear or anger from Him. Let it out. God can take it.

DAY 231

Stop lying there on the ground! Get up!
—*Joshua 7:10*

God heard Joshua's complaint, and He commanded him to take action.

There is a time for venting, a time for honest communication, a time for feeling your feelings. And then there is a time to stand up and step forward.

God wanted to communicate to Joshua the reason for the defeat at Ai. Joshua assumed God was at fault and blamed Him for the defeat.

But God revealed that accursed things had been taken from the enemy and kept hidden. Achan had sinned. And that sin had to be dealt with. Suddenly, it all became clear to Joshua. He knew what to do. And he would do it.

You may have times you need to dwell for a while on your feelings of pain or loss or grief. To work them through with grace to completion.

But there are also times to stop, get up, put the past behind you, and take positive action. Is this one of those times? Get up!

The LORD your God told his servant Moses that you were to kill everyone who lives here and take their land for yourselves. We were afraid you would kill us, and so we tricked you into making a peace treaty.
—Joshua 9:24

The Gibeonites were shrewd. They came to Joshua acting as though they had traveled from a far country, asking to make a peace treaty with Israel. Joshua did agree to make a peace treaty. But soon the Gibeonites' deception was revealed. They were close neighbors of the Israelites and would have faced destruction at their hands.

With the treaty, however, they had to be spared. Their deception did cost them their freedom, however. They became slaves of Israel. But they were willing to serve in order to keep their lives.

So, does deception work at times? Even though they deceived Joshua, he kept his word. A promise made with others should be kept, no matter what.

Joshua captured the land, just as the LORD had commanded Moses, and Joshua divided it up among the tribes. Finally, there was peace in the land.

—*Joshua 11:23*

For all intents and purposes, the land was Israel's. The Israelites had moved in and taken control. Joshua would apportion the land as he had been instructed. And the inheritance of the land was given to each tribe. Just as God had promised.

"Finally, there was peace in the land." The nation could spend some time settling down, resting, and enjoying the promised blessing. Yes, much turmoil awaited the people. But it was time to get recharged, restored, and refreshed.

Does that thought appeal to you today? Perhaps you need to take a break from the battles you're involved in at work, home, church. The challenges can seem insurmountable, and much work awaits.

But it has been given into your hand. And perhaps you need now to rest for a while. Declare peace.

DAY 234

Any one of you can defeat a thousand enemy soldiers, because the LORD God fights for you, just as
he promised. Be sure to always love the LORD your
God.

—Joshua 23:10–11

J oshua had the stage for his final words to the
people of Israel. He encouraged them to be
strong and courageous. To obey the word of the
Lord. To avoid false gods. To hold fast to the one
true God.

After all, He drove out the other nations. No
one could stand up to the might of the Lord and
the nation of Israel.

In fact, God's power was so great through
them that one Israelite could chase a thousand
away. Because it wasn't really the one Israelite
scaring them off. It was God Himself.

Joshua exhorted them: God deserves our love.
Our constant devotion. Our loyal relationship
with Him. Our obedience. Our standing firm for
His will.

He is exhorting us today, too.

Worship the LORD, obey him, and always be faithful. Get rid of the idols your ancestors worshiped when they lived on the other side of the Euphrates River and in Egypt.

—Joshua 24:14

You can't serve more than one God. The Israelites had had a history of not understanding that. As far back as Egypt, even on their journeys to the Promised Land, many of them maintained false religions and worshiped false gods.

But Joshua encouraged the people to show reverence and respect toward the Lord God alone. To obey and serve Him openly, honestly, truly—without any shade of deception or hiding from Him, which is fruitless anyway.

It's time, he said, to obey God, and God alone.

How would it look in your life to obey God? To make a conscious, concerted effort to be and do what He has called you to be and do?

Can you answer His call today?

But if you don't want to worship the LORD, then choose right now! Will you worship the same idols your ancestors did? Or since you're living on land that once belonged to the Amorites, maybe you'll worship their gods. I won't. My family and I are going to worship and obey the LORD!

—Joshua 24:15

The Israelites faced a lot of options. They had scores of gods to choose from. They could pick the kinds of gods that appealed to them. That made them feel good. That met their particular need.

There was only one problem. All those other gods were human ideas, often put into object form. They had no power, wisdom, or even true existence. So the people could serve those gods all they wanted. And they'd get nowhere.

Joshua demanded that they make their choice. To us, it seems a simple one. If you want power and truth and joy and peace, there is only one God. Are you part of Joshua's family? Will you worship and obey the Lord with your whole heart?

And so, I'll stop helping you defeat your enemies. Instead, they will be there to trap you into worshiping their idols.

—Judges 2:3

The angel of the Lord appeared to the people to chastise them for their disobedience. God had commanded them to clean out the land from all the influences of false religions. But they didn't obey.

As a result, the Lord said He would not force the pagans out of the land. Their false gods would trip up the Israelites continually.

If only they had obeyed. What peace might they have experienced? What fulfillment and joy in following God in their new homeland? But because they had not, they would be forced to deal with the enemies ready to trap them for the rest of their days.

Disobedience has its natural consequences. Sin can be forgiven—and is—but its results can affect us for the rest of our lives.

Remember that the next time you face a temptation to sin.

When enemies made life miserable for the Israelites, the LORD would feel sorry for them. He would choose a judge and help that judge rescue Israel from its enemies. The LORD would be kind to Israel as long as that judge lived.

—Judges 2:18

Israel entered a new phase of national life. The people had no king, but needed some kind of cohesive leadership to help deal with the enemy peoples who surrounded, oppressed, and harassed them. So God raised up judges for them. God was established as the Leader of the nation; the judges acted in response to His will.

God felt sorry for a group of people who continually ran away from Him. Scorned Him. People who broke His commands. Broke their promises. And broke His heart. Yet time after time He extended fresh grace to them, with the heart's desire that they turn to Him once and for all.

That's grace from the hand of the God who loves you, too, and will stick with you through all your problems.

Thus let all Your enemies perish, O LORD! But let those who love Him be like the sun when it comes out in full strength.

—Judges 5:31 (NKJV)

Deborah the judge sang a song of praise to rejoice over the victory of the nation Israel. This benediction caps the song—a plea for God to destroy the pagan enemies and let the people of God flourish.

You are familiar with the image here. The sky has been overcast for days. The gloom is depressing. Your spirit is drenched.

Then the skies start breaking up. The sun peeks out tentatively. Hinting at its power, but withholding it. Until finally the clouds are brushed aside. The sun shines stronger. Hotter. Brighter. The light blazes in all its glory and strength. Illuminating your world, shedding its bright and cheerful light.

That is a picture of the people of God in right relation with Him. It can be a portrait of you as well. Shine today in God's strength.

Please don't take this wrong, but if the LORD is helping us, then why have all of these awful things happened? We've heard how the LORD performed miracles and rescued our ancestors from Egypt. But those things happened long ago. Now the LORD has abandoned us to the Midianites.

—Judges 6:13

Again the Israelites fell into waywardness. And God allowed the pagan Midianites to overcome them. For seven years they were deeply oppressed.

God raised up another judge to deliver them. Gideon was the answer to the Israelites' cries. But despite an encouraging visit from the angel of the Lord, Gideon—like the whole nation—felt abandoned by God.

Yet, in truth, God had been abandoned by the nation.

The angel of the Lord told Gideon to go in his strength—and God's—and deliver the nation. God was there all along. He never left.

You may also suffer stretches of time when God seems to have disappeared. But God hasn't left. He's patiently waiting for you to turn back to Him.

"No," Gideon replied, "I won't be your king, and my son won't be king either. Only the LORD is your ruler."

—*Judges 8:23*

The people thought Gideon was doing such a good job as a judge, he ought to become the king of the nation. After all, the other nations had kings. Why couldn't they be like everyone else?

Gideon wasn't flattered, however. He knew that Israel's Lord was King. And that is the way it should be: a nation at peace with others and itself under the lordship of God.

Of course, it didn't last long. Kings would arise and fall. And ultimately, the nation—pursuing its own will rather than God's—would split and fall and be scattered.

We may have presidents and kings and prime ministers today. But there is only One who truly rules and reigns over all: the God who is the Lord of your life.

Is He truly your King today?

You've left me and gone off to worship other gods. If you're in such big trouble, go cry to them for help!

—Judges 10:14

The children of God had gotten themselves into trouble again. In pain and fear they cried out to God, confessing their sin, begging for His deliverance.

God could have let them wallow in their own will. In fact, He said, "You pursued other gods, so why aren't you asking them for help? Why aren't they saving you? Why do you always come running back to Me when you get in trouble?" The point was clear: The gods they pursued were powerless. They couldn't deliver the people from their distress. They weren't even alive.

The result was repentance once again. The people acknowledged what they had done and genuinely sought God's will for them. Whatever it was to be.

God still heard. God still answered. Their hard-heartedness hadn't stilled His love for them.

Please remember me, LORD God. The Philistines poked out my eyes, but make me strong one last time, so I can take revenge for at least one of my eyes!

—Judges 16:28

S amson was set apart from before his birth as a Nazirite—one wholly dedicated to God. He ruled with wisdom and courage and strength. Until he met his downfall in Delilah.

The enemies of Israel, the Philistines, had schemed and plotted to overtake Samson. And in his humanity, he eventually fell right into their hands. His supernatural strength—direct from God—was lost when his vow was broken for him not to shave his head. He was captured. And his eyes were plucked out as a final humiliation.

But he died with the Philistines in the temple by pushing the pillars aside. One last act of a brave saint who illustrated the follies of being human and being blessed by God. If you could do only one more thing on earth, what would it be? What would you need from God to accomplish it?

DAY 244

In those days Israel wasn't ruled by a king, and everyone did what they thought was right.

—*Judges 21:25*

The final words of the book of Judges echo a statement made more than once in the book. It was an indictment of the people of Israel during the time of the judges. They had no king. They did only what they thought was right.

They forgot their King was the God of the universe. And their forgetfulness led only to increasing suffering at the hands of their enemies.

But the Israelites are no exception to this human rule of thumb. God lavishes His blessings on us, leads us on a path of wholeness and joy, and then we wander off on our own way, in our own strength, in our own wisdom, and end up getting stuck in the mud or falling off a cliff.

Then we cry out to Him for deliverance, and in His grace He hears us.

Is that the pattern of your life? God invites you to break it. To walk closely with Him in His power and wisdom rather than your own.

Please don't tell me to leave you and return home!
I will go where you go, I will live where you live;
your people will be my people, your God will be my
God.

—Ruth 1:16

The situation was tragic: A woman who had lost
her husband to death years earlier now had lost
her two sons. She was alone. Only her daughters-
in-law remained, and she encouraged them to go
home to their own families.

One did. The other stayed. Her name was
Ruth. Her mother-in-law, Naomi, was returning
home to Bethlehem from Moab. And Ruth
would go with her.

Often couples recite these words in their marriage ceremonies to illustrate their commitment
to each other. They are beautiful words of devotion. Yet they weren't originally spoken of the
strong bonds of marriage. They reflect a choice
Ruth made freely and willingly and wholly.

This is the highest form of love and friendship
and family relations. Have you made a commitment like this to anyone?

DAY 246

I pray that the LORD God of Israel will reward you for what you have done. And now that you have come to him for protection, I pray that he will bless you.

—*Ruth 2:12*

Boaz had kept a special eye on Ruth. He provided her food from his fields and other necessary provisions. Filled with thanks, she exclaimed, "Why do you even notice me? After all, I'm a foreigner."

Boaz replied that he'd heard of her faith and devotion, her willingness to come to a strange land to help her mother-in-law. Then he offered this blessing on her.

Under the influence of her husband's family, Ruth came to believe in the God of Israel. And she sought refuge in Him. She made major sacrifices. She willingly gave up some of her rights to do what she felt was right.

And she had been given a blessing that God would see and hear and reward her for her loving actions. She had come to the right place for protection. It is always right to run to God.

SEPTEMBER 2

"Who are you?" he asked. "Sir, I am Ruth," she answered, "and you are the relative who is supposed to take care of me. So spread the edge of your cover over me."

—Ruth 3:9

Ruth's mother-in-law encouraged her to go to Boaz in the night as he slept on the threshing floor, uncover his feet, and lie down there.

Boaz was Ruth's relative. In that day, when a woman's husband died, her nearest male relative was responsible to marry her and care for her. He would be a kinsman redeemer.

Ruth did as her mother-in-law instructed. And in the night, Boaz awoke with a start to find a woman lying at his feet.

"Who are you?" he asked. And she answered with what amounted to a request for him to marry her. The story ended with their marriage. But that was not the real end of it. For they had children. And one of Ruth and Boaz's descendants was King David. Ultimately, from Ruth's line would come the Messiah, Jesus Christ. What might have happened if Ruth had not followed her heart?

You may go home now and stop worrying. I'm sure
the God of Israel will answer your prayer.

—1 Samuel 1:17

Hannah desperately wanted a son. So much so
that she was willing to give him to the Lord. She
came to the temple to pray and to make a vow to
God. Eli, the high priest, saw her. Her agony was
so great, her prayers so intense, he thought her to
be drunk and chastised her.

But she explained that she had been pouring
out her soul to the Lord in grief and anguish.
Hearing that, Eli blessed her and sent her away in
peace. Her prayer would be answered.

Prayer can change things. Sometimes we pray
by force of habit without really feeling our
prayers. Other times we come to God in desper-
ation and anguish, begging Him to hear and answer.

How have your prayers been lately? Are you
letting your feelings out with God? Are you per-
sistent in asking for what is important to you?

You make me strong and happy, LORD. You rescued me. Now I can be glad and laugh at my enemies.

—*1 Samuel 2:1*

Hannah sang a song of praise to the God who had answered her prayer for a son. Samuel was God's answer, and as she had promised, Hannah dedicated him to the Lord. He would live with God at the temple, serve Him all his days. And she was delighted that she could have such an important part in the life of her nation.

Her prayers had been answered. Her dreams had come true. Yet the joy in her heart was not over her son, but over her Lord.

He is a God who hears and answers prayer, whose word is life, and whose life is joy. He is a God who lifts up those from disgrace to honor. He is a God who offers victory over enemies and salvation over death.

Hannah had experienced all that for herself. She had seen God at work. She had been part of an awesome display of His magnanimous grace and mercy.

And hasn't He done the same for you? So how will you sing to your God today?

I can tell those proud people, "Stop your boasting! Nothing is hidden from the LORD, and he judges what we do."

—1 Samuel 2:3

In her song of praise, Hannah pointed to the God who had answered prayer so miraculously. He is the One who did it all. He is the only holy, powerful, and stable One in the universe. Therefore, take no credit for any success you may experience. Speak not of your own glory or ability. Give honor to the One to whom it is due, the only One who knows all and judges all. The One who is the source of all that is good and true and right and just.

Hannah knew the world was full of pretenders and self-important egotists. And she knew that all of them ultimately met an ignominious end. But she offered an opposing example: one who in humility acknowledged the true Source of all blessing and truth and power.

The world is short of saints like that and overcrowded with vain pretenders. Whose example will you purpose to follow today?

Our LORD, you are the one who makes us rich or poor. You put some in high positions and bring disgrace on others. You lift the poor and homeless out of the garbage dump and give them places of honor in royal palaces.

—1 Samuel 2:7–8

*S*overeignty. That's not a word we bandy about much these days. It brings to mind fairy tales with kings in faraway realms. Or we hear of modern-day royalty as sovereigns over their countries. Politicians speak of the sovereignty of nations in the world. But all of it pales in the face of the ultimate Sovereign: the Lord of all.

Sovereignty refers to the ability, authority, and power to declare what is to be and have it happen. Hannah spoke of the sovereignty of God when she pointed to Him as the One who establishes our circumstances and changes them as He wills. The poor, the rich, the high, the low—all are there for a purpose.

He can lift up; He can make strong. He did for Hannah. He did for so many others you've read about. He can for you. He is sovereign. Trust Him.

DAY 252

I have chosen someone else to be my priest, someone who will be faithful and obey me. I will always
let his family serve as priests and help my chosen
king.

—1 Samuel 2:35

A prophet came to the high priest, Eli, with a
word of God. It wasn't good news. Eli's sons had
misused their authority, and they would pay for
it. Their half-hearted service would put an end to
Eli's priestly line.

But God would raise up for Himself a faithful
priest who would talk with Him, obey Him, and
live for Him. Through this priest, God would
work to establish the line through which His
anointed would come—David and his descendants, and ultimately the Messiah Himself.

There are no dead ends with God. In the face
of human weakness or stubbornness, He always
creates a detour to fulfill His will.

And you can depend on it today. God is still at
work. It will happen in the perfect time, in the
perfect way, to a perfect end.

SEPTEMBER 8

The LORD then stood beside Samuel and called out as he had done before, "Samuel! Samuel!" "I'm listening," Samuel answered. "What do you want me to do?"

—1 Samuel 3:10

It was a season of spiritual dryness. God's voice wasn't heard much under Eli's priesthood. Yet Samuel served faithfully as a young boy.

One night he rested in the temple and heard his name called. He ran to Eli. Eli responded that he hadn't called Samuel. The same thing happened again. Samuel heard his name, went to Eli, and discovered he hadn't called after all. The third time, Eli realized what was happening: The Lord Himself was calling the boy. He sent Samuel back to bed with instructions to respond to God's voice.

And he did. God called him again, and he responded obediently. Samuel exhibited a heart of pure obedience and servanthood. He was primed to hear God's voice and ready to obey it.

Is God calling you? Have other voices drowned Him out? Are you prepared to respond today? Are you listening?

Do everything they want you to do. I am really the one they have rejected as their king.

—1 Samuel 8:7

Samuel was distressed. He had devoted his life to serving Israel as a God-ordained judge, pointing the people to God, seeking their best in His will. And yet they still called for a king, as other nations had. A human leader they could follow rather than living under the rulership of God. Samuel felt like a failure. His ideals had been rejected. And he took it personally.

But God reminded him that it wasn't Samuel they were rejecting. It was God Himself. They were rebelling against His rulership. And that was certainly not new behavior for the people of Israel. God was prepared to give the people what they wanted—as well as the consequences that would come along with it.

You've no doubt felt the same as Samuel at times. Rejected, unwanted, as though you were fighting an incoming tide. Listen to God. He can use the circumstances—and the tide—to change things.

The people would not listen to Samuel. "No," they said. "We want to be like other nations. We want a king to rule us and lead us in battle."

—*1 Samuel 8:19–20*

Samuel warned the people once again of the consequences of having a human king. He enumerated the points: A king will take your sons to battle. A king will require hard work of numerous people. He will tax you. Ultimately, he will cause you to cry out for relief—and the Lord will not answer you.

They knew the consequences. They refused to hear them. They wanted to be like other nations. They wanted their own king.

Who in their right minds would choose a weak human to lead them rather than follow the all-powerful God of the universe? Who in their right minds would choose their own will over the will of the all-knowing, all-seeing, all-loving One? Who, indeed?

The Spirit of the LORD will suddenly take control of you. You'll become a different person and start prophesying right along with them. After these things happen, do whatever you think is right! God will help you.

—1 Samuel 10:6–7

Samuel anointed Saul king of Israel. And with God's word, he explained what Saul would face in the days ahead. The primary event would be the coming of the Spirit of the Lord on Saul. Endowing him with God's power, wisdom, and strength. Filling him with God's word.

And with the Spirit of God infilling him, he would be turned into another man. He would be different. New. Unique. He would be himself fully realized, in the power of God.

That same power is available to you today. As a believer in Jesus Christ, you are indwelt by the Holy Spirit. He is the source of all power, wisdom, and strength. You can be a different person in Him.

Let me ask this. Have I ever taken anyone's ox or donkey or forced you to give me anything? Have I ever hurt anyone or taken a bribe to give an unfair decision? Answer me so the LORD and his chosen king can hear you. And if I have done any of these things, I will give it all back.

—1 Samuel 12:3

Samuel presented the new King Saul to the nation. And in doing so, he offered himself as an example of one who served faithfully, lived honestly and purely, and stood before the people unashamed. Not only did his life validate the selection of Saul as king, but it offered Saul an example of a leader who could lead in God's Spirit, follow God's will, and walk unashamedly after God.

Could you do the same? Could you stand before all your family, friends, coworkers, and neighbors and invite their charges? You can draw on God's power today to overcome any shame, and to empower you anew.

DAY 258

If you and your king want to be followers of the
LORD, you must worship him and do what he says.
Don't be stubborn!

—1 Samuel 12:14

Samuel gave the people a prescription for success in living: Worship the Lord. Serve Him.
Obey Him. That's nothing new. The people had
been exhorted to do that since the early days of
their existence.

But the situation had changed. They had a
human king. And both the people and the king
were responsible to follow closely after the Lord.

The situation had changed, but the rules
hadn't. God was still the ultimate sovereign over
the nation and her king. And if the people's eyes
were taken off God and moved to the king, they
would ultimately get stuck in the mire.

These commands are awesome responsibilities. But in truth they are gracious invitations to
a life of peace, power, and provision. A life that
offers fulfillment and serenity. A life that is abundant with joy and strength. A life that can be
yours today.

SEPTEMBER 14

Even though what you did was wrong, you don't need to be afraid. But you must always follow the LORD and worship him with all your heart. Don't worship idols! They don't have any power, and they can't help you or save you when you're in trouble.

—1 Samuel 12:20–21

In his coronation address, Samuel chastised the people for longing for a king. God finally granted them their wish, but it was not His will. And they would experience consequences for their choice.

Samuel's words stirred up repentance and sorrow among the people. They pleaded for mercy and acknowledged their sin. They asked Samuel to intercede for them, lest they die at God's hand. And Samuel offered the consoling words of today's verses.

You see, there is forgiveness in God's hand. Even when His children rebel against Him, even when we stubbornly withstand His will, He will offer a new beginning in His grace. Don't be afraid. Keep your eyes on the Lord, and there will be no reason to.

DAY 260

I would be disobeying the LORD if I stopped praying for you! I will always teach you how to live right.

—1 Samuel 12:23

As Samuel, the aging prophet and judge, spoke to the people at Saul's coronation, he pledged his own support to the people.

He would continue to serve as God's man, praying for them, teaching them, exhorting them. They committed themselves anew to follow after God, and they would indeed need prayer and instruction.

Samuel considered it a sin against the Lord for him not to pray for them. And prayer had to come before teaching "how to live right."

That's a fresh reminder of the significance of praying for others in our lives. As a spouse, parent, friend, coworker, neighbor, fellow worshiper, and more, each of us has ample opportunities to lift up those who are important to us in prayer.

To ask God to give them the strength they need to face their battles in life. To seek their growth personally—in body, mind, and spirit. To build them up in the knowledge and grace of the Lord.

What better time than now to do just that.

SEPTEMBER 16

Only fear the LORD, and serve Him in truth with all your heart; for consider what great things He has done for you.

—1 Samuel 12:24 (NKJV)

Samuel summarized the obligation of the people of Israel: "Only fear the LORD, and serve Him in truth with all your heart." But how can we fear God? After all, doesn't the New Testament say perfect love casts out fear?

There are two kinds of fear. The fear that terrorizes us—based on old memories or behaviors—is unhealthy. It restricts. It cuts off. It hurts. Fear of the Lord is, ironically, without that kind of negative fear. This fear is freeing, healing, upbuilding. It is coming to the almighty God of the universe in purity and openness, acknowledging His character and power, yearning to know Him better.

This kind of fear is a lifelong pursuit. Clear your mind of negative connotations of fear when you approach God.

But no, you disobeyed, and so the LORD won't choose anyone else from your family to be king. In fact, he has already chosen the one he wants to be the next leader of his people.

—1 Samuel 13:14

King Saul's actions looked good and right, but they were not God's will. He presumed they were. And in doing what he thought was right, he disobeyed God's word to him. He thought he knew better. And that pride would bring him down. It would end his dynasty without a single heir holding the throne of Israel.

Rather, Samuel said, the Lord was seeking "a man after His own heart" (v. 14 NKJV). Such a man would ultimately assume command of the nation.

God seeks those who want to know Him. Learn about Him. Follow after Him. Those who share His heart—a heart full of wisdom, grace, mercy, justice, love. He seeks those whose life goal is to pursue Him and, in the pursuit, to live in a way that reflects His will.

Saul has stopped obeying me, and I'm sorry that I
made him king.

—1 Samuel 15:11

Once again King Saul disregarded God's command and did what he thought was smarter and
better. Instead of utterly destroying the pagan
Amalekites and all their possessions, he spared
the king and the best sheep and cattle.

It made sense from a human perspective, but
it was not God's will. And that event sealed Saul's
doom.

So God spoke these words to Samuel. They
tore at the prophet's broken heart.

Saul's fate was cast; and yet he cast it himself.
His prideful, stubborn heart that continually ignored God's will led to his downfall.

Certainly, God was grieved. And God grieves
over every stubborn heart.

Because it could be so much better. If only we
would listen to God and accept His word. If only
we could live our lives by His power and grace
rather than trying to make it work ourselves. If
only we would trust God.

Does the LORD really want sacrifices and offerings?
No! He doesn't want your sacrifices. He wants you
to obey him.

—1 Samuel 15:22

Saul got defensive when Samuel asked why he
disobeyed God's command regarding the
Amalekites. He maintained that he *had* obeyed
God. He wiped out the Amalekites—all but the
king and the best sheep and cattle. But that was
to do even better than God had commanded, he
said, for the sheep and cattle would be sacrificed
to God.

So, he may not have completely obeyed God.
But he did better—and he did it for God.

But Samuel's response put things into perspective. Sacrifices meant nothing if they were offered with a disobedient heart, if they were
devoid of the devotion God seeks.

It's easy to get tied up in all our ritualistic responsibilities as humans, as children of God.
And lose sight of the primary goal that should
drive our lives: obeying God.

Rebelling against God or disobeying him because you are proud is just as bad as worshiping idols or asking them for advice. You refused to do what God told you, so God has decided that you can't be king.

—1 Samuel 15:23

The sentence was declared: Saul's rebellious heart would result in his removal as king.

Saul's sin may not appear to us to be that devastating. He didn't murder anyone. He didn't get involved in occult practices. He didn't worship idols. But Samuel explained that the sin of rebellion was the heart of the matter. Because it tore at the heart of Saul's relationship with God.

Saul's acts of disobedience in effect put his will above God's. And that was totally unacceptable to God.

God desires a heart that pursues Him, that yearns to do His will, that seeks to be with Him at all times. The kind of heart you want yours to be.

Samuel, I've rejected Saul, and I refuse to let him be king any longer. Stop feeling sad about him. Put some olive oil in a small container and go visit a man named Jesse, who lives in Bethlehem. I've chosen one of his sons to be my king.

—1 Samuel 16:1

There is a time for grieving, and there is a time for moving on.

Samuel was devastated by Saul's fall from God's favor. Imagine the investment he had made with his own life. He had anointed the man, advised him, prophesied to him, supported him, chastised him. He was like a father. But Saul had been rejected for his rebellious heart.

God had grieved (see 1 Sam. 15:35). Samuel was free to grieve as well. And yet there comes a time to take action and move on with life. Samuel would anoint God's chosen king.

Ask God if you're ready to move on today, too.

DAY 267

Don't think Eliab is the one just because he's tall and handsome. He isn't the one I've chosen. People judge others by what they look like, but I judge people by what is in their hearts.

—1 Samuel 16:7

Saul was strong and tall and handsome. He looked the part of a king.

Faced with Jesse's boys, Samuel wondered what God was up to. One after another, the sons were dismissed. Until none was left. Oh, yes, the youngest boy was out in the fields tending the sheep.

Samuel had seen Jesse's son Eliab—a tall, strong man—and assumed he was God's choice. No, God said. Don't look at his outward appearance. Look at the heart. That's how God chose David. He looked at his heart and found one that yearned to follow Him.

You can never know a person's heart as well as God does, but you can be sensitive to another's soul. You can sense the spirit within.

SEPTEMBER 23

DAY 268

A man named Jesse who lives in Bethlehem has a son who can play the harp. . . . He's a brave warrior, he's good-looking, he can speak well, and the LORD is with him.

—1 Samuel 16:18

Saul was deeply troubled. God's Spirit had left him; he was tormented by evil.

His attendants suggested bringing in someone who could play the harp to soothe his soul and bring peace. Saul agreed, and he asked them to find someone who could play skillfully. One servant answered with today's words. Unknown to him, the future king of Israel would come to serve the fallen king.

The servant's description of young David was enthusiastic. What better description could there be?

The truth is, the last description—"the LORD is with him"—was the key to the first descriptions. It wasn't David they were describing, but the Lord working through David. So you don't have to force yourself to meet some ideal. Just open yourself up to a creative, powerful, winning Lord. He is willing to work through you.

DAY 269

The LORD has rescued me from the claws of lions and bears, and he will keep me safe from the hands of this Philistine.

—1 Samuel 17:37

Goliath the Philistine. His presence brought weaker men to their knees in fear. And Israel had to put its whole weight behind a single individual to go hand to hand with the giant nemesis. Who would go?

David—the young shepherd boy, the skillful musician to the king—volunteered. King Saul reacted with surprise because of David's youth and size.

But David defended himself. As a shepherd, he had fought for the lives of his sheep from out of the clutches of lion and bear. And if he could succeed with those enemies, he could certainly do battle with a mere human—giant though he was.

And Saul couldn't argue. He said, "Go ahead and fight him. And I hope the LORD will help you" (v. 37).

True self-confidence comes only when our lives are established in God. David was actually God-confident. And that's the only confidence that truly wins.

SEPTEMBER 25

DAY 270

You've come out to fight me with a sword and a spear and a dagger. But I've come out to fight you in the name of the LORD All-Powerful. He is the God of Israel's army, and you have insulted him too!

—*1 Samuel 17:45*

Goliath the Philistine was insulted. The Israelites sent a boy to fight him, without armor, without weapons, without a chance.

Where was the sport in that! He laughed with contempt. It would be quick and easy work, and he would feed the boy's flesh to the birds.

But David spoke up: "You may be loaded up with all sorts of physical weapons, but I'm carrying a power far greater than all the weapons of the world. I come in the name of the Lord, the God of our entire nation. And that means you've bitten off far more than you could ever chew."

It's an old saying that one plus God can equal anything. And nothing is impossible with God. It's true. Find out for yourself today.

DAY 271

David and Saul finished talking, and soon David and Jonathan became best friends. Jonathan thought as much of David as he did of himself.

—1 Samuel 18:1

Jonathan and David. One of the classic friendships of all time. Two souls bound together as brothers in the Lord.

And the fact that David would become the next king of Israel, Saul's successor, made the friendship more remarkable. Because by natural right, the job was Jonathan's as Saul's rightful heir.

But Jonathan's heart for the Lord was pure, too. He knew God had called David, and he honored it. Rather than considering the crown something he lost, Jonathan considered David's value as a person, friend, and future king to be a far greater gain.

Think of the images in this verse: "The soul of Jonathan was knit to the soul of David, and Jonathan loved him as his own soul" (NKJV).

Wouldn't you like to have a friendship on that level? Perhaps God will bless you with a friend like that. Perhaps He will equip you to be a friend like that.

SEPTEMBER 27

Take care of yourself. And remember, we each have asked the LORD to watch and make sure that we and our descendants keep our promise forever.

—1 Samuel 20:42

David's life was in jeopardy. King Saul was a madman, determined to put his successor to death, thwarting God's plan.

Saul's own son ran interference for David. According to a prearranged plan between the friends, Jonathan went out to where David was hiding. He signaled to David secretly that David's life was in grave danger.

The friends were able to meet briefly to say goodbye: "Then he and Jonathan kissed each other and cried, but David cried louder" (v. 41). Then Jonathan pronounced this blessing on David.

You've probably had some good friendships that have been broken because of distance and time. Remember the support and joy you received from them?

Today, touch base with someone special with whom you've lost contact. See what the Lord has done in his or her life.

We're not going to attack Saul. He's my king, and I pray that the LORD will keep me from doing anything to harm his chosen king.

—1 Samuel 24:6–7

David had his chance to destroy Saul and assume his rightful throne. He was there, unknown by Saul. He could have easily run the king through with his sword. In fact, he cut a piece of Saul's robe as proof of his restraint.

Why not end it all and hasten what was God's will? David couldn't do it. Saul had been anointed by God to be the king. How could he possibly hurt the anointed of the Lord?

Of course, God had already withdrawn from Saul. David had already been anointed. Yet David's respect and reverence for the office of king—under the authority of God—were unshakable. He had standards to keep. It was an easy way out, but David wouldn't take it.

You'll face more than one "easy way out" today. Remember David when you do.

DAY 274

They cried all day long and would not eat anything. Everyone was sad because Saul, his son Jonathan, and many of the LORD's people had been killed in the battle.

—2 Samuel 1:12

King Saul, severely wounded with arrows, died by his own sword during a battle with the Philistines. His three sons—including Jonathan—also lost their lives at the same place and time.

The king was dead. Long live the king! But David was in no hurry to assume command. First would come a time of grief.

It was a bitter, sad end to a strange chapter of Israel's history. But it was behind them. God's anointed, David, could rule with a strong heart, mind, soul, and body in the power of God.

Major change is never easy. The loss of a family member, a move, a career change, starting over—it takes time to adjust. Time to grieve the loss. Time to prepare for the new challenges.

Give yourself the time you need today.

SEPTEMBER 30

It was easy to love Saul and Jonathan. Together in life, together in death, they were faster than eagles and stronger than lions.

—2 Samuel 1:23

David lamented the deaths of King Saul and his son Jonathan in a song. He pointed to the love and respect they enjoyed. Their strength and abilities as leaders and as men.

Yes, David had had his struggles with Saul. Yet this was a time to remember the good that his life brought to so many.

Jonathan may have opposed his father Saul in many ways. But in death, he chose to stand with his father and die by his side. Their reconciliation was forged on that hill at the point of a sword.

Certainly, David grieved over the death of his closest friend. Theirs was a special relationship and one that would live forever.

David sang, "Jonathan, I miss you most! I loved you like a brother. You were truly loyal to me, more faithful than a wife to her husband" (2 Sam. 1:26).

Death can put things into perspective. It can force us to recognize the value of our relationships. Don't wait for death to make you realize it.

We are your relatives. Even when Saul was king, you led our nation in battle. And the LORD promised that someday you would rule Israel and take care of us like a shepherd.

—2 Samuel 5:1–2

Though David had been anointed king over all Israel and Judah, Saul's heirs attempted to wrest control. That brought about a war between the houses of David and Saul, with Ishbosheth ruling over Israel and David over Judah.

The intrigue continued—until Ishbosheth and his advisors were ultimately put to death. Then, representatives from Israel came to pledge allegiance to David. They recognized that David was truly an Israelite. There may have been division and war, but the blood lines prevailed. And most important, they recognized that God Himself had placed David in authority over them as their shepherd and ruler.

Like them, we can surrender and acknowledge God's choice for us. We can stop trying to force our will and open ourselves to His. It's amazing what can happen when we do.

[David] was dancing for the LORD with all his might, but he wore only a linen cloth. He and everyone else were celebrating by shouting and blowing horns while the chest was being carried along.

—2 Samuel 6:14–15

The chest, or the ark of the covenant, was returned to the possession of the Israelites, and David was gloriously happy. He began leading the procession by dancing before the Lord in joy and abandon. He may not have acted with kingly dignity, but he couldn't help himself.

David's wife looked at her husband dancing so recklessly, and she despised him for his undignified behavior. When she expressed her displeasure, David had no excuse but one: "The LORD didn't choose your father or anyone else in your family to be the leader of his people. The LORD chose me, and I was celebrating in honor of him" (v. 21).

If we can be free, open, and honest with ourselves, we too can offer our lives to the Lord with joyful abandon.

Go to David and give him this message: . . . "Why should you build a temple for me?"

—*2 Samuel 7:5*

Nathan the prophet received the word of God one night. It came to Nathan after David expressed his concern that the ark of the covenant of God resided in a mere tent, while he lived in a palace of cedar. It didn't seem right to him.

So God responded through Nathan. God desired that His people experience some stability and security regarding their worship of Him. He wanted a permanent home with His children. But it was not yet time to build a temple. It was time to fight the battles to secure the land. It was time to establish peace in the kingdom. And that would require all of David's attention.

Even the prophet Nathan voiced his approval of David's idea. It wasn't until Nathan heard God's word that night that His will was clearly revealed.

Don't second-guess God. Don't assume you know what God wants of you. Seek out His will. He may have a surprise in store for you.

I'll choose one of your sons to be king when you reach the end of your life and are buried. . . . I'll make him a strong ruler, and no one will be able to take his kingdom away from him. He will be the one to build a temple for me.

—2 Samuel 7:12–13

David received a wonderful promise from God in the light of his disappointment over not being able to build a temple for His dwelling. There would come a time when a temple would be built. It would come under the reign of David's son. His line would continue. The kingdom would be established.

God's plan would unfold deliberately. It would take time. It would need the proper context—a kingdom secure under the authority of David and his descendants. But it would happen.

God has our best interests at heart. His plan for our lives is unfolding. We may not know the details. But we can trust that it's happening as we walk with Him.

I will be his father, and he will be my son. When he does wrong, I'll see that he is corrected, just as children are corrected by their parents. But I will never put an end to my agreement with him, as I put an end to my agreement with Saul, who was king before you.

—2 Samuel 7:14–15

God's promised blessing of David extended to his unborn son. He would be a son not only to David but also to God Himself. And when he fell into sin, God promised to discipline him, but He also promised not to remove His mercy from him.

God had taken away the blessing from Saul, but He would not remove it from David's son. And surely, no promise is sweeter to a father than the eternal pledge of grace and favor for his children.

You are just as much a child of God as Solomon would be. God will chasten you when you walk away from His path. And that chastening may hurt. But He will never remove His mercy from you. He will never leave you or forsake you.

LORD All-Powerful, my family and I don't deserve
what you have already done for us.

—*2 Samuel 7:18*

Kfing David went to the tent of meeting and
sat before the Lord. He couldn't believe what was
happening to him. He was the king of Israel, the
anointed of God. He was the recipient of un-
fathomable grace and favor. He had been
promised immense power and glory that would
last for generations. And his son would be even
more blessed than he.

His response was amazement: What have I
done to deserve this?

That's a common response for one who has experienced and basked in the love and grace of
God. For one who has recognized the price God
paid to enter into an eternal relationship with
him. For one who takes advantage of the privi-
lege of knowing and serving God.

What have I done to deserve this? Nothing.
Absolutely nothing. Which makes it all the more
amazing.

And there is no other nation on earth like Israel, the nation you rescued from slavery in Egypt to be your own. You became famous by using great and wonderful miracles to force other nations and their gods out of your land, so your people could live here.

—2 Samuel 7:23

Israel was a nation composed of people pretty much like any other people. They lived, worked, ate, fought, argued, served, worshiped. They were men and women and boys and girls with needs and pains and joys and sorrows and faults and good points.

They were just like us. They did nothing special on their own to earn God's favor. They were chosen by God to be redeemed and to be a witness to other people.

David recognized this truth: "You have chosen Israel to be your people forever, and you have become their God" (v. 24).

Just as God worked with the Israelite nation, He works with us individually. He chose us for a purpose. And He wants to reach the world through us.

Is He able to work out His purposes through you today?

I wonder if any of Saul's family are still alive. If they are, I will be kind to them, because I made a promise to Jonathan.

—2 Samuel 9:1

David sought out a relative of Jonathan to whom he could show kindness and favor. He learned of a son of Jonathan named Mephibosheth. He arranged to bring him to the palace to live with his own family.

Can you imagine Mephibosheth's feelings at being called before the king? Mephibosheth couldn't believe it. What had he done to deserve such generous treatment? Nothing. It was a matter of love and honor and respect.

David's heart can warm our own to reach out to others because of our love. And in that reaching out, we can reflect the gracious, abundant love of God for us. For He, too, invites us to fellowship with Him every day. To be His honorary children. To share in His abundance. Because of His love.

DAY 284

Be brave and fight hard to protect our people and the cities of our God. I pray that the LORD will do whatever pleases him.

—2 Samuel 10:12

David's general Joab was sent to battle the Ammonites. He called the troops together for a pep talk and encouraged them to fight bravely.

His words echoed God's frequent encouragement in the Old Testament to be strong and brave. To face the battle, the difficult circumstances, strong in the confidence of God, determined to do the best you can do, filled with purpose and hope.

Then the Lord would do what pleased Him.

We do our part, and God will take care of it. No matter what happens, we can know that it is God's will. It is what seems best to Him. It is His sovereign plan.

You may prove victorious. You may be injured. You may even be defeated. But it is in God's hands. And all He asks you to do is enter the contest courageously in His strength. Then no matter what happens, you will win. Because God's will moves forward, and you are part of it. Remember that as you face today's battles.

The sacred chest and the armies of Israel and Judah
are camping out somewhere in the fields with our
commander Joab and his officers and troops. Do
you really think I would go home to eat and drink
and sleep with my wife? I swear by your life that I
would not!

—2 Samuel 11:11

David succumbed to the temptation of a beautiful woman, voyeuristically watching her and
wanting her and arranging to meet her. And in so
doing, he broke more than one of the Ten Commandments. For not only did he covet and take
his neighbor's wife—resulting in her pregnancy—but he arranged to have her husband
killed.

He tried to bring Bathsheba's husband, Uriah,
home from the battlefront so it would appear as
though he had caused her pregnancy. But Uriah
was a man of principle, and he would not leave
the troops. So David sent Uriah to the front lines
to his certain death.

It all started with a look. It ended in a national
tragedy. Be careful where you look today. God
can give you the strength you need to look away.

You are that rich man! Now listen to what the LORD God of Israel says to you: "I chose you to be king of Israel. I kept you safe from Saul."

—2 Samuel 12:7

The Lord sent Nathan the prophet to David. David thought he had it all figured out, his tracks covered, everything taken care of.

Bathsheba was his; her husband was dead; the war was over.

And Nathan told a story of two men. One rich, the other poor. The rich man had innumerable sheep and cattle; the poor man had only a single ewe lamb. A lamb that had become his children's pet, a member of the family. It ate his food, drank from his cup, and even slept in his arms. When the rich man had a visitor, he decided rather than kill and prepare one of his sheep, he would have the ewe lamb of the poor man. David burned with anger. "That man deserves to die!" he blurted to Nathan.

"You are that rich man!" Nathan rebuked the king, thrusting the spear of truth into David's heart. David had all that he could possibly need, but he took Bathsheba and killed her husband.

The truth can hurt deeply. Search your heart. Examine your motives and desires. Before it becomes too late.

DAY 287

David said, "I have disobeyed the LORD." [And Nathan said,] "He has forgiven you, and you won't die."

—2 Samuel 12:13–14

An ice-cold slap. A revelation of incredible sin. David felt it with Nathan's rebuke. He had planned his sinful steps so carefully. It could have worked.

But God saw and knew all. And through Nathan, He opened David's eyes to his desperate sin.

David's heart hadn't hardened. Immediately, he opened up to the truth: "I have disobeyed the LORD." His heart was obedient, honest, and open to God. The sin had not yet frozen it. And as a result, there would be consequences, but the sin would be forgiven by God.

There will be times we will sin. That is a fact of human life. And in those times, we can build our defenses and harden our hearts.

Or we can open our hearts and eyes and watch God work in us.

While he was still alive, I went without food and cried because there was still hope. I said to myself, "Who knows? Maybe the LORD will have pity on me and let the child live." But now that he's dead, why should I go without eating? I can't bring him back! Someday I will join him in death, but he can't return to me.

—2 Samuel 12:22–23

As part of the consequence for his sin, David would suffer the death of the child of his sinful relationship with Bathsheba. When the child became ill, David pleaded for him. He fasted and prayed. On the seventh day, the child died. David's servants feared his reaction to the news.

But David's attitude changed. Once God had made His will clear with the death of the child, there was no need to pray. God had acted; the outcome would not change.

Fervent prayer makes sense when God's will is in question. He welcomes it. But when God acts, it is time to be reconciled with reality. It is time to move on.

My son Absalom! My son, my son Absalom! I wish I could have died instead of you! Absalom, my son, my son!

—2 Samuel 18:33

Years after the death of David's infant son by Bathsheba, another son, Absalom, would die. David's grief was bottomless. Absalom had shown great promise. But he had ultimately led a rebellion against his father in an attempt to wrest the throne from him.

It was one of the darkest, most difficult chapters of David's reign. His life was at grave risk—and all at the hand of his son.

When Absalom was killed, David was deeply shaken. The grief over his son's death was no doubt exacerbated by the rebellion. There was no opportunity to reconcile. No opportunity to experience the relationship as it should have been.

There is a time for grief, and there is a time for acceptance. There is a time to release emotions, and there is a time to get life back on track. What time is it for you?

DAY 290

Our LORD and our God, you are my mighty rock my
fortress, my protector. You are the rock where I am
safe. You are my shield, my powerful weapon, and
my place of shelter. You rescue me and keep me from
being hurt.

—2 Samuel 22:2–3

In a song of praise, David worshiped the Lord,
recognizing His character and attributes, His
abilities and works.

My rock. Strong, steady, firm, unbreakable. *My
fortress.* A place of protection from harm, a place
to do battle with the outside world that seeks to
tear apart and destroy. *My protector.* He rescues
us from harm and difficulty. He brings us into
peace.

My shield. Nothing can get to us without His
permission. He keeps us from being hit by the
ammunition of the world and the devil. *My place
of shelter.* He is a place to go to replenish our supplies, to build our resources, to experience perfect safety and protection.

Strength, security, stability, peace—all are
available in Him. Today.

Death, like ocean waves, surrounded me, and I was almost swallowed by its flooding waters. Ropes from the world of the dead had coiled around me, and death had set a trap in my path. I was in terrible trouble when I called out to you, but from your temple you heard me and answered my prayer.

—2 Samuel 22:5–7

Death. Sorrows. Pressures. Distress. Pain. Fear. We confront these demons daily. Sometimes they pass; other times they burden us for what seems an eternity.

David experienced them. And when he did, he called on the Lord. He cried out to God.

And God heard from heaven. And hearing the cry, He acted.

If you're feeling as though you're drowning in pain, cry out. And know that God will hear you. And answer.

On the day disaster struck, they came and attacked, but you defended me. When I was fenced in, you freed and rescued me because you love me.

—*2 Samuel 22:19–20*

David was surrounded by enemies, both real and intangible. His life seemed a disaster. Everything was falling apart. And he was cornered by his pain. Boxed in, pressed down, claustrophobic in his misery.

But the Lord defended him. David could trust in the protection of God. In the Lord was everything he needed to survive and to thrive.

God rescued David. Why? Because He loved him.

In the same way, God loves you, cares for you, is concerned for you. He yearns to lift you up and set you free. He wants to give you the strength and wisdom you need. He wants to raise your spirits, open your eyes, set you on solid ground, empower you.

DAY 293

You are good to me, LORD, because I do right, and
you reward me because I am innocent.

—2 Samuel 22:21

David isn't bragging about his righteousness
here. Certainly, he had committed his share of
sins.

Nor is David saying that God measures out
blessing according to our goodness, as if we were
being paid for the positive things we do.

Rather, David is pointing out a fundamental
truth of life: God rewards people who earnestly
seek Him and desire to follow Him.

When we make it the priority of our lives to
know Him, our lives will shine with righteousness, truth, and honesty. We will be different
from the world. Our eyes become His; our
hands, His hands; our hearts, His hearts. Our
lives will be changed. Our actions become a natural outflow of our relationship with Him.

If you feel shortchanged in the blessings de-
partment, don't question God's motives; examine
your heart.

OCTOBER 19

DAY 294

Our LORD and God, you are my lamp. You turn darkness to light.

—*2 Samuel 22:29*

Darkness. You can't see. You stumble around, stubbing your toe, knocking your shin, falling down.

Darkness is fear. Insecurity. Confusion. Ignorance. Powerlessness. Death. Nothingness.

Darkness is life apart from God. The sun may shine, but our hearts remain dark. Our lives black with pain and sin.

But look to God, and the light comes on. It floods our souls, warms our hearts, brightens our spirits.

Light is hope. Security. Confidence. Strength. Warmth. Power. Wisdom. Life. Truth.

God is light. He lights our paths. He shines on our lives. He shows us the way. Bask in His light today.

OCTOBER 20

You are my strong fortress, and you set me free. You
make my feet run as fast as those of a deer, and you
help me stand on the mountain.

—*2 Samuel 22:33–34*

Sing with David today. Proclaim your feelings
about God. Praise Him for what He has done
and is doing.

He is your strong fortress. Without Him,
where would you be? How would you cope?
How would you handle the pain and fear of life?
How would you fulfill your calling? How could
you even get out of bed in the morning?

He gives you everything you need if you're
open to it. The strength to face your daily challenges, the power to overcome in His Spirit.

He makes your feet like a deer's—swift, powerful, free. He leads you up to the mountain to
marvel at His works, His creation, His life of
freedom and purpose.

He sets your feet on solid ground, so you can
experience security and trust.

He alone can do all this. He is worthy to be
praised. Sing to Him today.

**You are the living LORD! I will praise you! You are a
mighty rock. I will honor you for keeping me safe.**
—2 Samuel 22:47

When all was said and done, when David
looked back over his life, when he reviewed his
accomplishments and his glories, one thing stood
out: God had done it all. God lives and reigns
and moves and shakes the world.

God lives and gives life. God puts all things
right, raises holy things up, tears ungodly things
down.

God is the Ruler, the Achiever, the Giver, the
Blesser, the Lover, the Fighter, the Empowerer.

And this realization of God's work in his own
life leads David to praise.

The Lord is alive and living and working in
your life. Do you see Him? Do you know Him?
Do you sense His hand of guidance on you?

Look back and see the path you've been walking. Realize where you've come from. And acknowledge the growth that God has given you on
the way.

I will soon die, as everyone must. But I want you to
be strong and brave. Do what the LORD your God
commands and follow his teachings. Obey everything written in the Law of Moses. Then you will be
a success, no matter what you do or where you go.

—*1 Kings 2:2–3*

David knew his days were numbered. So he
gave his son Solomon, who would follow him as
king, words of fatherly advice. The strength he
called for isn't inherent male strength. It is God's
strength. And it is available to everyone. The
bravery involved putting trust in the Source of all
strength.

God placed His hand of destiny on Solomon's
shoulders. The walk ahead wouldn't be easy, but
if he would take those steps with God, he would
have no problems. It was a question of obedience. The choice was Solomon's.

Relying on God's strength for the journey, following His will in the way, would lead to a life of
true success: a life overflowing with peace, purpose, and power.

David's words still echo. You, too, can respond
to them in obedience and trust.

DAY 298

Solomon loved the LORD and followed his father
David's instructions, but Solomon also offered sacrifices and burned incense at the shrines.

—*1 Kings 3:3*

Solomon's heart was right. He loved the Lord.
He walked in the path his father David had
blazed. There was just one thing: He "offered
sacrifices and burned incense at the shrines."
That opened the door to spiritual weakness.

Solomon was doing the right things, but in
the wrong place. The shrines were altars abandoned by false religions. The Israelites were forbidden to use them to worship the one true God.
Worshiping in those places tended to open the
Israelites to the influence of the false gods. And
Solomon would repeatedly stumble in that area
throughout his reign.

Question your motives. Examine your heart.
Are you doing the "right things" in the wrong
way or with the wrong person or at the wrong
time? Is it affecting your integrity, your honesty,
your openness with God?

LORD God, I'm your servant, and you've made me king in my father's place. But I'm very young and know so little about being a leader. . . . Please make me wise and teach me the difference between right and wrong. Then I will know how to rule your people. If you don't, there is no way I could rule this great nation of yours.

—1 Kings 3:7, 9

Most scholars believe Solomon was about twenty when he assumed the throne of Israel. Imagine how overwhelmed you would feel in Solomon's sandals as you faced the prospects ahead.

It made Solomon feel like a little child. He felt totally unprepared for the task. Even the simple things of life seemed hugely intimidating.

But Solomon revealed a trait that would mark his whole life: wisdom. Wisely, he asked God to give Him an understanding heart to judge His people. To discern good and evil.

Without God's help, the task was impossible. With God's wisdom, in God's power, anything was possible.

It still is. It just depends on what you pray for.

I'm pleased that you asked for this. You could have asked to live a long time or to be rich. Or you could have asked for your enemies to be destroyed. Instead, you asked for wisdom to make right decisions. So I'll make you wiser than anyone who has ever lived or ever will live.

—1 Kings 3:11–12

Solomon was preparing to become king of Israel. He could have expected God to provide wealth and victory and honor and all the other things kings are privileged to enjoy. But he didn't ask for them. Instead, he asked for wisdom and understanding in order to rule fairly and well.

It was a genuine request, full of humility and reality. And God heard it. In fact, Solomon's request seemed to touch His heart in an unusual way. He answered with far more than Solomon asked for.

Our requests in prayer say a lot about us. God's answers to our prayers say a lot about Him. So what are your prayers saying? And how is God answering?

DAY 301

Everyone in Israel was amazed when they heard how Solomon had made his decision. They realized that God had given him wisdom to judge fairly.

—1 Kings 3:28

Two prostitutes came to seek justice from the king. Both lived in the same house. Both had infant sons, but one of them died in the night. Each argued that the living child was her own.

Solomon surely startled them with his command: "Bring me a sword. . . . Cut the baby in half! That way each of you can have part of him" (vv. 24–25).

His command had its intended result: The true mother begged the king to give the son to the other woman in order to spare his life. The false mother demanded the death of the baby to settle the dispute. Solomon had gotten his answer, shrewdly, wisely.

God will give wisdom if we ask Him for it (see James 1:5). The world needs more wisdom. Will you be a channel for it today?

The LORD God promised my father that when his son became king, he would build a temple for worshiping the LORD. So I've decided to do that.

—*1 Kings 5:5*

The time had come to fulfill the dream of building a temple.

King Hiram of Tyre, a friend of Solomon and of Israel, sent his envoys to the king. Solomon responded that he was ready to start construction on the temple, and he needed Hiram's help.

Peace reigned; God had given the nation rest under Solomon. No adversary, no disaster required his attention, so he could focus on the temple.

The two kings worked in peace for years to come. The temple would indeed be built.

Timing is everything. When God's time is right, the pieces fall into place. The needs are met. Peace reigns. It works out.

DAY 303

Suddenly a cloud filled the temple as the priests were leaving the most holy place. The LORD's glory was in the cloud, and the light from it was so bright that the priests could not stay inside to do their work.

—1 Kings 8:10–11

Only the best materials were used for the temple. Finally, after seven years, the day had come to finish it. The ark of the covenant was carried in and set in place. The priests came out of the Holy of Holies, and suddenly, the Lord's glory filled the place. They were overwhelmed by the magnitude and brilliance of God's glory. They couldn't continue their work, so great was the glory that filled the temple.

God seemed overjoyed to enter His new home with His people. So overjoyed, He couldn't contain Himself. He was ready to receive their worship and praise, ready to give them what they needed. God fills human hearts the same way—when they are prepared, open, ready for Him. Invite Him to overwhelm you today with His glory.

There's not enough room in all of heaven for you, LORD God. How could you possibly live on earth in this temple I have built?

—1 Kings 8:27

In his prayer of dedication, Solomon put things into perspective. Yes, they had built a magnificent structure for the Lord. Yes, He had filled the temple with His glory. But that didn't mean Israel had God in a box.

Just because He was present with them in a powerful way in the building didn't mean He wasn't everywhere throughout the world, just as powerful and present.

Israel may have built a beautiful temple, but the people didn't have exclusive rights on God. And Solomon realized that. Not even the whole of the planet, the entire universe, could contain God's majestic power.

God chose to bless His people through their temple. But He was far, far more than a cloud in a building.

It's easy to box God into preconceived notions or expected responses. Open your false box today. Open your whole world to His power and presence.

Listen when anyone in Israel truly feels sorry and sincerely prays with arms lifted toward your temple. You know what is in everyone's heart. So from your home in heaven answer their prayers, according to the way they live and what is in their hearts.

—*1 Kings 8:38–39*

Whenever any child of God made a sincere request, Solomon begged God to hear. To forgive. To act. To give. To deal with each person according to the heart.

God will know the sincere prayer. He will know the heart that desires to follow Him. And He will respond accordingly.

God—and God alone—knows your heart. He knows your need. He knows your sincerity and your desire. Turn to God for relief. And realize that God will hear the cries of the soul that lives life genuinely, hopefully, and humbly.

If any [foreigners] pray toward this temple, listen from your home in heaven and answer their prayers. Then everyone on earth will worship you, just like your people Israel, and they will know that I have built this temple to honor you.

—*1 Kings 8:42–43*

God was the God of Israel. He had chosen the people specifically to be His children. But His love and concern were not exclusive. In fact, He chose the Israelites to be a channel of His love and grace to the whole world.

So Solomon prayed that God would hear even foreigners' prayers. And by hearing and answering, let the whole world know that He is indeed God, and that all peoples would fear Him.

God is not exclusive. No single group of people can claim Him as their own. He created the whole world and everything in it. Including every person. He yearns that everyone know Him. Personally. How could you be part of that process today?

Answer them when they pray toward this temple I have built for you in your chosen city, here in this land you gave their ancestors. From your home in heaven, listen to their sincere prayers and do what they ask.

—1 Kings 8:48–49

When God's people sin, Solomon prayed, may God hear them.

Solomon had a realistic view of one of our primary struggles in life: the tendency to sin. To shirk responsibility. To turn away from what we know is right to do something we think will be better.

Solomon recognized that it was a real possibility for the Israelites to sin to the point of experiencing God's wrath by being taken captive. Yet they could repent. And God could hear. And so it was done.

So let it be done today. If you are struggling with sin, turn to God. He will hear. He will forgive.

DAY 308

Then on the eighth day, he sent everyone home. They said good-by and left, very happy, because of all the good things the LORD had done for his servant David and his people Israel.

—1 Kings 8:66

The temple was dedicated to God and filled with His presence. Solomon prayed a moving prayer for his people. And it was a glorious time. For eight days they celebrated the completion. They prayed and worshiped and learned about God. They sang and cheered and danced with joy. Finally, Solomon had to send them away.

Accomplishing a major achievement, reaching a major milestone, is cause for celebration. Perhaps there's one in your life. A significant step forward in your personal growth. The restoration of an important relationship. A victory in ministry or service.

Don't let it slide by without recognizing the accomplishment—and seeing God's hand in it. Celebrate it. Let gladness fill your heart. Praise the Lord for it.

And you'll be filled with new vigor and energy for the next accomplishment.

NOVEMBER 3

As Solomon got older, some of his wives led him to worship their gods. He wasn't like his father David, who had worshiped only the LORD God.

—1 Kings 11:4

Solomon loved many women, and that led to his downfall. His wives came from many foreign countries—marriages no doubt made as part of political relationships with the other nations.

In fact, he had seven hundred wives of royal birth and three hundred concubines. And they led him away from the God of Israel. With so many foreign women, he couldn't help being influenced by their pagan ways. As a result, his heart grew cold to the one true God.

Distractions abound in your world, too. You're surrounded by temptation constantly in the world, at work, through the media. Not only sexually, but philosophically, spiritually, and intellectually. The influences may be very subtle at first, but they build and grow and deepen. Unless you maintain strong boundaries and a solid foundation.

But Jeroboam kept on doing evil things. He appointed men to be priests at the local shrines, even if they were not Levites. In fact, anyone who wanted to be a priest could be one. This sinful thing led to the downfall of his kingdom.

—1 Kings 13:33–34

Jeroboam became king of Israel through sinister plotting and subterfuge. His whole life exhibited a calculated disdain for God and His ways. His degradation reached the point that he gave away priesthoods to anyone who wanted them. The problem was, very few of the men were godly. And this sin was so abominable to God that He intended to exterminate Jeroboam's line from the face of the earth.

We may be horrified at such spiritual corruption. But spiritual complacency is a primary problem of the church today. Focus on the reality of your relationship with God. Tap into His power and presence, and know your faith is alive and well.

Abijam did not truly obey the LORD his God as his ancestor David had done. Instead, he was sinful just like his father Rehoboam.

—1 Kings 15:3

King Abijam walked the path of sin and separation from God. His heart was not bound to God, as David's had been.

But what about David's sin? How was he any better than Abijam?

David's sin was a matter of his humanity. And he humbly admitted his wrong and sought God's forgiveness and cleansing when he realized what had happened.

Abijam's sin was calculated. His heart was set against God.

God will receive the heart that is humble and repentant. When we sin, we know He will hear our pleas to forgive. A loyal, devoted heart can lead to a life of blessing and honor and joy. A cold, dead heart that willfully excludes God will lead only to tragedy and destruction.

The choice is yours.

And [Ahab] set up a sacred pole for worshiping the goddess Asherah. Ahab did more to make the LORD God of Israel angry than any king of Israel before him.

—1 Kings 16:33

The spiral downward into degradation continued to lead the nation deeper into the mire. Ahab, king if Israel, was the latest spiritual disaster. As leader of the nation, he even established Baal worship as an official religion. As a result, he provoked the Lord's anger to burn even hotter.

Ahab's soul was a vacuum, sucking up anything it could get apart from the Lord God. He had no guilt, shame, or feeling of loss. Right and wrong meant nothing to him—only what seemed best to him set the standard for his behavior.

As sin infuses our lives, it deadens us to God's will. As we continue our pursuit of personal pleasure, our hearts are walled up against God's gracious Spirit.

It's a long, slow, torturous process. The result is spiritual deadness. The first step is a single decision to ignore God in perhaps one small area of life.

Guard yourself against taking a step like that today.

Leave and go across the Jordan River so you can hide near Cherith Creek. You can drink water from the creek, and eat the food I've told the ravens to bring you.

—1 Kings 17:3–4

Elijah. His name means "the Lord is my God." A refreshing truth rarely heard in his land at the time. God raised him up to oppose the worshipers of Baal among God's people. The king of Israel, Ahab, was actively promoting the pagan ways, and God had had enough.

God led Elijah away from the land and people for a while, thereby totally removing His presence and His power from their midst. For the sinful people there would for a time be no hint of God. They suffered famine and drought. But God provided all of Elijah's needs.

Perhaps God has taken you aside for a while for some purpose you may not fully understand. He will meet your needs there. He will strengthen you and provide His word for you. You can depend on Him.

You are God's prophet! . . . Now I know that you really do speak for the LORD.

—1 Kings 17:24

God led Elijah to Zarephath, where a widow with a son would provide him with food and water. But her provisions were low. So, miraculously, God provided more than enough for them to eat during the drought and famine plaguing the land.

Later, the woman's son became ill and ultimately died. The woman was distraught. Elijah took the dead boy and cried out to God. He asked God to restore the boy's life. And God heard his prayer. Joyfully, he brought the living boy to his mother.

How quickly we forget! Why do we doubt in the face of trouble? Why do we think God may be punishing us unjustly through some painful circumstance—an assumption that ignores all His benefits and blessings that we've enjoyed? God may raise our sons, or He may not. But He is still God. And we can trust Him, no matter what.

When he saw him, Ahab shouted, "There you are, the biggest troublemaker in Israel!" Elijah answered: "You're the troublemaker—not me! You and your family have disobeyed the LORD's commands by worshiping Baal."

—1 Kings 18:17–18

The evil king Ahab had it backward. The nation was suffering from drought and famine. When he saw Elijah, God's prophet, approaching, the king blamed Elijah as the cause of all Israel's troubles.

But Elijah set Ahab straight. He was merely the instrument of God's judgment, not the cause of it. The cause was Ahab's rebellion against God.

God's power can be troubling to those who draw back from it. God's truth can be upsetting to those who refuse to believe it. God's love can be repulsive to those who are caught in the bonds of sin. And God's grace can be turned back by those who cannot believe it is offered genuinely.

You can be a bearer of God's power, truth, love, and grace today. Be prepared to make some waves.

DAY 316

Elijah stood in front of them and said, "How much longer will you try to have things both ways? If the LORD is God, worship him! But if Baal is God, worship him!" The people did not say a word.

—*1 Kings 18:21*

God was prepared to do battle with the forces of Baal. First, Elijah set the choice clearly before the people. It was either God or Baal. They could no longer play with both. They had tried to maintain ties to their religion, playing it safe, while pursuing the more enticing ways of the false gods.

But the people couldn't make a choice. They stood in silence.

We can't have it both ways. We can't pursue God in an intimate relationship with Him and pursue the ways of the world at the same time. We can't live His way and our way simultaneously. We can't obey Him while seeking ways to get around His truth. We can't live with a divided heart.

There comes a time to choose. To be committed. To take a stand. To close one door and walk through the other.

NOVEMBER 11

Our LORD, you are the God of Abraham, Isaac, and Israel. Now, prove that you are the God of this nation, and that I, your servant, have done this at your command. Please answer me, so these people will know that you are the LORD God, and that you will turn their hearts back to you.

—1 Kings 18:36–37

Elijah had set forth the contest. Each group would call on the name of their deity, and whoever "answers by starting the fire is God."

The followers of Baal had done their best. They sacrificed a bull. From morning till noon they called on Baal to consume it. They leaped in a frenzy. Nothing happened.

Then it was Elijah's turn. He rebuilt an altar to the Lord. He offered his own bull sacrifice. He doused it thoroughly with water. Then he prayed. All that was a last-ditch effort to get the people's attention, to force them to see the truth, to show where true power could be found. Elijah was used by God mightily so that the people might see and know Him.

What if you prayed and asked God to make Himself known through your efforts?

[Elijah] walked another whole day into the desert. Finally, he came to a large bush and sat down in its shade. He begged the LORD, "I've had enough. Just let me die! I'm no better off than my ancestors."

—1 Kings 19:4

On top of Mount Carmel, God showed Himself strong. The Lord showed without question that He was the one true God.

The people saw what happened, fell on their faces, and declared, "The LORD is God! The LORD is God!" (1 Kings 18:39).

The prophets of Baal were executed. The drought was ended. But evil rulers Ahab and Jezebel were not happy. They issued a death warrant. And Elijah ran for his life.

In the face of overwhelming victory, he hid in the wilderness and prayed that God would just go ahead and get it over with.

Who hasn't reached that point? When you do, acknowledge it, and let it go. Pray about it. God will hear you, just as He heard Elijah.

All at once, a strong wind shook the mountain and shattered the rocks. But the LORD was not in the wind. Next, there was an earthquake, but the LORD was not in the earthquake. Then there was a fire, but the LORD was not in the fire. Finally, there was a gentle breeze.

—1 Kings 19:11–12

Elijah was full of fear, anxiety, depression over Jezebel's death threat, despite being a firsthand witness of God's awesome power.

God told Elijah to go out and stand on the mountain, for He was about to pass by. And Elijah witnessed a strong, destructive wind, a violent earthquake, and a consuming fire, but the Lord was not in any of them.

Finally, Elijah heard a gentle breeze, or a soft whisper, surprising in its peace and calmness. It was not time for violence or destruction. It was time for simplicity and peace and quiet strength.

Are you waiting for God? Are you expecting too much? Are you ignoring His quiet voice? Are you not listening hard enough?

After they had reached the other side, Elijah said, "Elisha, the LORD will soon take me away. What can I do for you before that happens?" Elisha answered, "Please give me twice as much of your power as you give the other prophets."

—2 Kings 2:9

It was time to pass the prophet's mantle on to the next generation. Elijah had taken Elisha under his wing. Elijah gave Elisha the opportunity to ask for whatever he needed.

And Elisha asked to be considered Elijah's firstborn son in the faith, inheriting his responsibility and his authority, along with the power behind it. The power of God.

Elijah responded that it was God's sovereign pleasure as to what would happen: "It can happen only if you see me as I am being taken away" (v. 10). Then a fiery chariot approached, and Elijah was swooped into heaven by a celestial whirlwind, into the very presence of God. God had answered Elisha's request.

Be bold in asking God for what you need to serve Him more completely, more powerfully. Then watch what happens.

"There's not enough here for a hundred people," his servant said. "Just give it to them," Elisha replied. "The LORD has promised there will be more than enough."

—2 Kings 4:43

There were still some faithful people in Israel. And rather than bring their offerings to the apostate priests of the land, they recognized Elisha as God's man and brought him their firstfruits to honor God.

One man brought ripened grain and some barley loaves and gave it all to Elisha. The prophet told his servant, "Give it to the people so they can eat" (v. 42). And, amazingly, they all did.

God had already demonstrated throughout Elijah's and Elisha's ministries that He was able to bring plenty where there was need. Through His own Son, Jesus, He would echo that truth—twice, in the feeding of five thousand and four thousand.

You may feel your resources are impossibly small to accomplish what you'd like. But God can give you everything you need and more. He can start with what you have and provide an abundance.

His servants went over to him and said, "Sir, if the prophet had told you to do something difficult, you would have done it. So why don't you do what he said? Go wash and be cured."

—2 Kings 5:13

Naaman was a great man. A commander of the Syrian army. An honorable leader. A mighty man of valor. But he was also a leper. An outcast.

He heard of Elisha's power and ability, and soon he was at Elisha's door, asking for his help. Elisha told him, "Go wash seven times in the Jordan River. Then you'll be completely cured" (v. 10).

Naaman was furious. That was too easy! But his servants encouraged him. And Naaman swallowed his pride and followed Elisha's instructions. And his flesh became as clean and pure as a little child's.

Sometimes God doesn't ask much of you. Sometimes you may ignore doing the simple things that could bring you so much joy and cleansing and power. Listen to God. Heed Him even in the little things.

DAY 323

Then [Elisha] prayed, "LORD, please help him to see." And the LORD let the servant see that the hill was covered with fiery horses and flaming chariots all around Elisha.

—2 Kings 6:17

The situation didn't look good. Elisha's servant discovered an enemy army had surrounded their city. Horses and chariots were poised for attack. And they were hopelessly outnumbered.

He ran back to his master: "Sir, what are we going to do?" (v. 15).

Elisha prayed for God to open the servant's eyes. And He did. The servant saw a mountain full of fiery horses and flaming chariots all around Elisha.

Elisha knew that in the power of God, there was greater strength than in any number of earthly horses and chariots. The unseen host of heaven was prepared to do battle for God's faithful few.

Thank God, His mighty host is fighting on our side. We don't see, but we can know. And we can prepare for the battle: "So put on all the armor that God gives. Then when that evil day comes, you will be able to defend yourself" (Eph. 6:13).

NOVEMBER 18

DAY 324

I, the LORD, command you to stop doing sinful
things and start obeying my laws and teachings! I
gave them to your ancestors, and I told my servants
the prophets to repeat them to you."

—2 Kings 17:13

Generation after generation, the Israelites ignored God, sinning against Him, pursuing other
gods, despite all that He had done for them.

God's patience is strong and long lasting, but
there is a limit. Even though in grace and mercy
He kept reaching out for His children, they kept
turning their backs on Him.

And now, the last call. One more time, God
urged them to repent.

"But the Israelites would not listen; they were
as stubborn as their ancestors who had refused to
worship the LORD their God" (v. 14).

It takes a strong person to yield to Him. To
hear and heed His call. To turn to Him in faith
and follow Him in truth. How strong are you
today?

Hezekiah trusted the LORD God of Israel. No other king of Judah was like Hezekiah, either before or after him. He was completely faithful to the LORD and obeyed the laws the LORD had given to Moses for the people.

—2 Kings 18:5–6

While Israel was having a last gasp of freedom before being taken captive by Assyria, Judah enjoyed a brief breath of fresh air under the reign of Hezekiah. A refreshing change: a king who trusted in the Lord God. A leader who held fast to Him. A man of God who obeyed the word of God: "The LORD helped Hezekiah, so he was successful in everything he did" (v. 7).

God can do much through the life of one obedient person. In Hezekiah's case, the odds were too great against him. The tide was virtually impossible to turn. The degradation of the people was virtually complete. But the fact that one so vulnerable to God could arise in that setting gives hope. It's never too late. It's never too little.

Don't forget that I have been faithful to you, LORD.
I have obeyed you with all my heart, and I do whatever you say is right.

—2 Kings 20:3

Hezekiah, the faithful king of Judah, was sick
and near death. Isaiah, the prophet of God, came
to him to say, "You are going to die, so you had
better start doing what needs to be done" (v. 1).

But Hezekiah wasn't ready. He didn't feel his
job was done. And he prayed to God for more.

Before Isaiah could leave the court, God gave
him a message for the king and said He would
heal the king and defend the city.

God gave His people in Judah one more
chance under a godly king. He delights to answer
prayers, giving us what we ask in humility and
with pure motives. And giving far more than
what we ask.

What prayer would you boldly pray today in
the spirit of Hezekiah?

[Hezekiah] told Isaiah, "The message you brought me from the LORD is good."

—2 Kings 20:19

Isaiah the prophet brought to King Hezekiah a pronouncement of God. And Hezekiah exclaimed that the message was good.

But wait a minute—what exactly was the pronouncement? "One day everything you and your ancestors have stored up will be taken to Babylonia. The LORD has promised that nothing will be left" (v. 17).

God announced through Isaiah that the nation would be cleaned out by the Babylonians. Nothing would be left.

Yet Hezekiah, knowing and trusting God, could still say that was "good." Because he knew God is God and His will is best.

What if God told you something devastating would happen to you? Would you be able to respond as Hezekiah did? Is your faith that strong, your trust that sturdy? Are you able to exult in God's will, no matter what it means to you personally?

I will even get rid of my people who survive. They will be defeated and robbed by their enemies. My people have done what I hate and have not stopped making me angry since their ancestors left Egypt.

—2 Kings 21:14–15

God's people would be delivered to their enemies. God's patience was exhausted. Since the days of Moses, they tried Him. They repeatedly chose evil rather than good. And they would suffer the consequences for their choices.

God is longsuffering and gracious, but He is a just and holy and righteous God. He cannot tolerate stubborn sin forever.

Ultimately, the people would return to the land. The Savior would come from the land. And in the end, the kingdom would be established in the land.

This isn't the end. It's a prelude to a new beginning. Even in judgment, there is hope. That's the kind of God He is. Thank Him for that.

DAY 329

The LORD must be furious with me and everyone else in Judah, because our ancestors did not obey the laws written in this book. Go find out what the LORD wants us to do.

—2 Kings 22:13

Josiah was a godly king. He did what was right in God's sight. After he had reigned eighteen years, at age twenty-six, he called on the nation to rebuild the temple that had fallen into disrepair. It was a metaphor for the nation's spiritual condition. It had to be fixed.

And in the process of repair, the high priest discovered the long lost Book of the Law, the first five books of the Bible. That, too, indicated that the people had strayed far from the truth in the intervening years.

Josiah had the Book read to him. And he tore his clothes in grief. Josiah realized that the nation had wandered far away from the will of God and he took steps to restore his nation as best he could.

You haven't lost God's Word. But do you read it, know it, and make it part of your daily life?

I noticed how sad you were when you read that this country and its people would be completely wiped out. You even tore your clothes in sorrow, and I heard you cry.

—2 Kings 22:19

 King Josiah's heart was broken when the Word of God was discovered and read to him. He realized the nation had been ignoring God's truth. His high priest Ahikam and others went to Huldah the prophetess, who gave them a word from God about the destruction of the country and the people.

But God had a special word for Josiah. Because he was tenderhearted, open to God and His word, and humble in its presence, God heard him: "So I will let you die in peace, before I destroy this place" (v. 20).

Everything depends on our individual relationship with God. No matter what's happening around us, no matter how degraded the world can be, the only truth for us is our relationship with Him. Strengthen your relationship with Him. He will honor your heart.

DAY 331

David met them outside and said, "If you are coming as friends to fight on my side, then stay and join us. But if you try to turn me over to my enemies, the God our ancestors worshiped will punish you, because I have done nothing wrong."

—*1 Chronicles 12:17*

Here we see King David's courage and strength in God. Early in his reign, as the army of Benjamin and Judah approached him at his stronghold, there was great doubt as to their motives. Would they attempt to overthrow the king and restore the house of Saul? Or would they come to join forces with him?

God knew their hearts. The Chronicler writes, "God's Spirit took control of [Amasai, chief of the captains,] and he said 'We will join you, David son of Jesse! You and your followers will always be successful, because God fights on your side'" (v. 18).

Stand strong. Make the challenge. God will take care of the rest.

DAY 332

"Should I attack the Philistines? Will you help me win?" The LORD told David, "Yes, attack them! I will give you victory."

—*1 Chronicles 14:10*

David had become king over all of Israel. The nation was united once again. And when the enemy Philistines heard the news, they went to find the new king.

Should David pursue them and enter into battle? Would Israel be victorious? He could have agonized over those questions. But his first step was to pray. To ask God to show him His will. To seek out direction from the only One who could truly give it. And God promised victory.

How quickly do we react to the circumstances in our lives as David did? Do we get bogged down in fear and worry, trying to figure out what to do with our incomplete understanding and knowledge? Do we try to do what seems right or what others tell us would be smart? Or do we immediately go to God and ask Him?

DAY 333

Praise the LORD and pray in his name! Tell everyone what he has done. Sing praises to the LORD! Tell about his miracles.

—1 Chronicles 16:8–9

The ark of the covenant was returned to its home. The people rejoiced. And David wrote a song to commemorate the victory.

"*Praise the LORD*." Realize the source of the blessing, and tell Him how you feel about that.

"*Pray in his name! Tell everyone what he has done*." Identify the source of your blessing and joy. Make Him known to those around you.

"*Sing praises*." Singing is the natural result of a heart filled with praise and glory. And when we recognize God's great blessing, we can't help telling others what He has done.

Spend some time today putting David's words into practice. Praise Him, pray, talk about Him, and sing to Him. He is worthy! He is God!

Celebrate and worship his holy name with all your heart. Trust the LORD and his mighty power. Worship him always.

—1 Chronicles 16:10–11

The people rejoiced. Their hearts burst with joy and celebration. All was right in their land. It was time to give thanks.

Good times give us an opportunity to seek God afresh. To build a stronger bond with Him. To dedicate our hearts again to Him. For there will come a time when we are despondent and seemingly alone. When God doesn't seem to hear us. When we are overwhelmed by obstacles and adversaries, fears and frustrations, pain and powerlessness. Building a stronger relationship with God beforehand, in times of strength and joy, can prepare us for the difficult times. And they become part of the cycles of life. The ups and downs, the joys and sorrows, all of it surrounded and supported by a strong relationship with God.

Remember his miracles and all his wonders and his fair decisions. You belong to the family of Israel, his servant; you are his chosen ones, the descendants of Jacob.

—1 Chronicles 16:12–13

Remember God's miracles. Remember His wonders and His decisions. What is He teaching you? What lessons has He placed indelibly on your heart?

Bring those things to mind and cherish them. Write them down. Pray them through. That is a way to keep God's love and grace fresh in your mind and spirit. A way to give you strength to face the difficulties and frustrations of your day.

We forget far too easily. We ignore the multitude of blessings He has showered on us. We erase from our minds the lessons we've learned, the steps we've taken forward, the wounds He has healed, the gifts He has given.

Don't forget. Recall as many blessings and truths as you can. Life is full of them. He gives them in abundance. Receive them. Record them. Remember them. Recall them. Relive them.

DAY 336

He is wonderful! Praise him and bring an offering into his temple. Worship the LORD, majestic and holy.

—1 Chronicles 16:29

King David and his people were exultant. They cheered the return of the ark of the covenant. They honored the One who had given them the land and the blessings that came with it. They praised the God of the universe, who was their Lord.

In David's psalm commemorating the occasion, he called on the people to give God the glory. Realize who had accomplished the great victory. Take steps to acknowledge His work.

Nothing is more sublime than gathering together in good cheer to thank God for carrying out His will victoriously. Nothing is more meaningful than for a human soul to experience with other souls the splendor of God's holy presence.

God alone is worthy of our worship. He alone is due the recognition and the glory for His work in our lives. Today join with some fellow pilgrims and praise God for His wondrous works.

DECEMBER 1

Tell the heavens and the earth to be glad and celebrate! And announce to the nations, "The LORD is King!" Command the ocean to roar with all of its creatures and the fields to rejoice with all of their crops. Then every tree in the forest will sing joyful songs to the LORD. He is coming to judge all people on earth.

—1 Chronicles 16:31–33

All creation bursts forth in praise for its Maker. The heavens rejoice. The stars shine perpetually to honor Him. The vast oceans tell of His inexhaustible creativity and power.

The earth in its beauty and complexity reveals its gladness for being spoken into existence. God made it, He oversees it, He rules it, and He will judge it. The entire creation knows this is true. Everything that exists acknowledges God as the sovereign One—now and ultimately.

The only thing left is the human population. Each soul must individually acknowledge the place of God in the universe and in his or her life.

Nathan replied [to David], "The LORD is with you—do what you want."

—1 Chronicles 17:2

When David expressed his desire to build a temple, Nathan recognized his deep, heartfelt desire. He realized it was a genuine wish coming from a godly man. So he encouraged the king to do it.

But that night, God spoke to Nathan to tell him David would not be the one to build His temple. David had work to do in establishing the nation. God made it clear that David's desire would not be fulfilled in his lifetime.

The truth here is that we need to test our desires against God's desires. What feels right, what seems proper, may not be what God wants right now.

If you have a dream in your heart, and you're walking with God, it's vital to examine that dream and ask God if it is His as well. Pray, be open to God's leading, and be willing to lay down that dream if it isn't His best for you.

David was miserable and said, "It's a terrible choice to make! But the LORD is kind, and I'd rather have him punish me than for anyone else to do it."

—*1 Chronicles 21:13*

Ignoring God's will, King David called for a census of the nation as part of the preparation for building the temple. This presumptive act angered God. So when David realized his sin, he confessed his foolish act.

Through David's prophet Gad, God gave the leader a choice of punishment for the sin: three years of famine, three months of losses against enemies, or three days of plague from the hand of the Lord. David reached the point of surrender to God, thereby opening the way to a devastating plague.

In our distress because of our wrong choices, we can choose to run, or we can face the consequences in God's hands. David chose wisely. We can trust God to deal with us in perfect love and justice.

DAY 340

David prayed, "It's my fault! I sinned by ordering the people to be counted. They have done nothing wrong—they are innocent sheep. LORD God, please punish me and my family. Don't let disease wipe out your people."

—1 Chronicles 21:17

David took ownership of the guilt of his presumptive sin against God, and he asked the Lord to spare the people the effects of His justice.

God heard and led David to find the site of the future temple. It was a ray of hope in a dark and difficult time for the leader.

How stubbornly do you refuse to surrender to God in acknowledging your responsibility for your sin? How courageously do you stand up to face the music rather than blame someone else, society, or God Himself? Take responsibility. Own your part in what's happening in your life now. Ask God to show you how to learn from it and grow through it.

May he give you wisdom and knowledge, so that
you can rule according to his Law.

—1 Chronicles 22:12

A father offered his advice to his son. David
was nearing the end of his reign, and he counseled his son Solomon for the task ahead.

He acknowledged that it was his desire to
build a temple for God. But because David had
shed so much blood and fought so many wars,
God had made it clear that he was not the one to
build the holy temple. That would come under
the watch of his son, a man of peace and rest.

It must have been disappointing to David not
to have a direct hand in the building of the temple. Yet it must have been fulfilling to know he
prepared the way to enable his son to achieve the
long-held dream.

David exhibited true grace in accepting God's
will, and joy in his part of it. The glory would
come later, but he could be glad for it even then.

Is God trying to tell you something through
this character strength of David?

Obey the LORD your God with your heart and soul. Begin work on the temple to honor him, so that the sacred chest and the things used for worship can be kept there.

—1 Chronicles 22:19

David had planned and worked hard to prepare the way for his son Solomon to build the temple. Everything was in place. All was ready. It would fall on Solomon to do the work.

And it would require wholehearted devotion to accomplish. Solomon could not possibly carry out the job unless he fixed his heart, his soul, his whole being on the Lord. He would have to focus his whole life on one goal.

He had to start with his relationship with God. And when that was strong and sure and open and pure, only then could he do the work.

We get it backward so often. We plunge headlong into the tasks—many of them honorable and right—without fortifying ourselves first with God's strength, in tune with His will, open to His working within us and through us. Heed David's prayer today.

Solomon, my son, worship God and obey him with all your heart and mind, just as I have done. He knows all your thoughts and your reasons for doing things, and so if you turn to him, he will hear your prayers. But if you ignore him, he will reject you forever.

—1 Chronicles 28:9

The depth and intensity of David's fatherly advice to his son are touching. But it can be even more touching when you hear the words addressed to yourself.

"*Worship God . . . as I have done.*" David's walk with God was certainly not perfect, but his heart exhibited a depth of passion for God rarely witnessed.

"*Obey him with all your heart and mind.*" God fully knows the motives and thoughts that stand behind everything we do.

"*If you turn to him, he will hear your prayers.*" That is the great "if" of life. It is the most beautiful promise God has given us. David knew it to be true. You can, too.

Be confident, and never be afraid of anything or get discouraged. The LORD my God will help you do everything needed to finish the temple, so it can be used for worshiping him.

—1 Chronicles 28:20

Again, David spoke words of strength and encouragement to his son. And they can build strength and courage in us today.

Solomon faced an enormous task: leading an unruly people, pulling together all the loose ends of the kingdom, and above all building a magnificent temple worthy of the God of the universe. And Solomon was but a young man.

His father's advice echoed the word of God throughout the Old Testament. Find your confidence and courage in the source of all confidence and courage: God Himself.

But don't stop with that. David counseled, "Do everything needed." Do what He has given you to do. Without fear or discouragement. Because He will be with you continually, restoring you, replenishing you, renewing you.

I praise you forever, LORD! You are the God our ancestor Jacob worshiped. Your power is great, and your glory is seen everywhere in heaven and on earth. You are king of the entire world.

—1 Chronicles 29:10–11

David had done everything he could to prepare for the building of the temple of God. All that was left was for Solomon to oversee the work.

So David called his nation to pray. To thank God for what He was preparing in their midst. To turn their hearts toward the One who provided for every need, including spiritual growth. To praise Him for being their God, for living in their midst even without a temple to call home.

God created the world. He owns it, He loves it, He works through it, and He will bring it all to ultimate fulfillment. David's God is the same God you worship today. Let David's passion sweep you into the heavenlies today. Listen to the words. Feel them. Echo them. Reflect them back to God.

You rule with strength and power. You make people rich and powerful and famous.

—1 Chronicles 29:12

God is our source for all of life. Prosperity, power, provision—it all comes from His hand. He is sovereign in its distribution.

The problem is, when things are going well— your job is good and you're making the money you need, you're advancing in society, you're strong in your growth and health—it's easy to lose sight of that Source. We tend to think we did it all ourselves. That it was our intelligence and ability that brought our good fortune.

Recognize that God is sovereign. Any good thing in your life has come directly from His hand. You didn't cause it, you didn't earn it, and you can't necessarily keep it.

Recognizing that truth builds humility. Thankfulness. Honesty. And these are the characteristics that God truly delights in and blesses.

DAY 347

We are only foreigners living here on earth for a while, just as our ancestors were. And we will soon be gone, like a shadow that suddenly disappears.
—*1 Chronicles 29:15*

Without God, we are lost and wandering. Without God, our days are as a shadow—without substance, meaning, or significance. Without God, we are without hope. Life is mere existence. Our spirits are as deflated balloons, our hearts weak and empty.

But when we find God, things change. We have a path to walk. We have direction. We experience hope and peace and joy. Life becomes truly alive. Colorful. Noisy with joy.

You have experienced the distinction, haven't you? Yes, even with God there will be gray days, silent times, loneliness, lostness. But they are the exceptions. They are opportunities to let God's Spirit infuse you once again and fill you with all that He is. Feel the presence of God in your life.

LORD God of Israel, no other god in heaven or on earth is like you! You never forget the agreement you made with your people, and you are loyal to anyone who faithfully obeys your teachings.

—2 Chronicles 6:14

Solomon dedicated the new temple with a stirring prayer, leading his people to the throne of God. And he recognized the Lord God of Israel as the one true God.

Do you question where God is in your life? Do you wonder why your life is so meaningless, purposeless, or dry? Are you angry with God because things just don't seem to be going your way? Are you frustrated that you seem stuck in your personal growth? Are you overwhelmed by the pains of your past that keep haunting you and holding you back?

If you are plagued by such questions, ask yourself one more: Am I walking before God with all my heart?

Wholehearted love for God will change your life.

If my own people will humbly pray and turn back to me and stop sinning, then I will answer them from heaven. I will forgive them and make their land fertile once again.

—*2 Chronicles 7:14*

God explained how easy it would be to experience His blessing. And it all came down to a choice: The people could live His way or their own way.

His way meant humbling themselves. Confessing their sin, turning it over to Him, realizing their need for Him. It meant turning from their self-centered wickedness, no longer seeking pleasure and power outside His will.

His way meant praying and turning to Him. Desiring to be in His presence, communicating with Him about every part of life, yearning to live in His light.

And by living His way, they would have His grace and mercy, His healing and forgiveness, flowing through their lives.

The choice was simple. But God's people chose not to make it. What do you choose?

It belongs to me, and this is where I will be worshiped forever. I will never stop watching over it.

—2 Chronicles 7:16

At the dedication of the new temple, God spoke to assure His people that He had chosen and sanctified it. It was a structure worthy of His presence. So it was set apart from all other structures on earth. It was His home.

God would "never stop watching over it." He would always see and feel what His people were doing and saying. He would watch over them as a loving parent. He would be aware of their needs.

Today, we don't have a temple serving as God's dwelling place. But He dwells within each child.

Each of us is the temple of God's Spirit. He has taken up residence within us. And He watches over us continually. He sees; He feels what we see and feel. He knows us more intimately than anyone could.

The Lord is in His holy temple: you.

I praise the LORD your God. He is pleased with you and has made you king of Israel. God loves the people of this country and will never desert them, so he has given them a king who will rule fairly and honestly.

—2 Chronicles 9:8

The Queen of Sheba had heard great things about Solomon and his kingdom. So she came to find out for herself. She asked him hard questions. And he handled them all with wisdom. The reports she had heard about the king's achievements and wisdom were true, she stated. As a result, she praised the God of Israel, who had apparently delighted in Solomon and honored him with the throne of Israel.

Living God's way can make an impact on the world. Solomon's righteousness and wisdom provoked a response among the people of other lands. So much so that they acknowledged God's power and presence.

What do people see when they look at the way you live?

DAY 352

LORD God, only you can help a powerless army defeat a stronger one. So we depend on you to help us. We will fight against this powerful army to honor your name, and we know that you won't be defeated. You are the LORD our God.

—2 Chronicles 14:11

Asa was a good king of Judah. He did what was right and good in God's eyes. During his reign, the vast army of King Zerah of Cush (Ethiopia) came against Israel. The soldiers of God went out and prepared for battle.

But first, Asa prayed. The situation was overwhelming. The Cushites far outnumbered the Israelites. It didn't look good. Yet Asa knew that God could handle anything.

Israel rested in God. In His name the people went to battle. And they crushed the Cushites. The defeat was decisive.

How often do we face a crisis, start a project, or launch a ministry without calling on God's support and strength first? What would happen differently if we did next time? Perhaps today you'll find out.

DAY 353

For a long time, the people of Israel did not worship the true God or listen to priests who could teach them about God. They refused to obey God's Law. But whenever trouble came, Israel turned back to the LORD their God and worshiped him.

—2 Chronicles 15:3–4

Asa had been a godly king. But the nation was on a downward spiral. It was time to turn to God without the need. To live with Him in times of peace and prosperity.

Asa was encouraged by a word from Azariah the prophet: "So you must be brave. Don't give up! God will honor you for obeying him" (v. 7). He removed the despised idols. He restored the altar of God. And he called on the people to gather and make offerings to the Lord.

God is always there for you. In times of trouble and hardship, it's easy to turn to Him for help. But He wants to be your Lord at all times. There is always work to be done. And He will always give you the strength and courage to do it.

The LORD is constantly watching everyone, and he gives strength to those who faithfully obey him.

—*2 Chronicles 16:9*

In his later years, Asa's trust in God waned. Rather than believe that God would empower him and his people—as He had in the past, for example, when they went to war against Cush—Asa sought alliances with foreign pagan nations.

Hanani the prophet came to Asa to rebuke him for his lack of trust. The rebuke stung Asa. Angrily, he put the prophet in prison. His heart had gotten cold and hard.

Loyalty to God does not come naturally to us. We must keep our hearts open and vulnerable to Him. Or we can subtly slide out of His will. And before we know it, we're in alliances with the world.

Don't let that happen. Be aware of your heart condition. Know that God is searching constantly for your loyal heart, and He is ready to show Himself strong in your life if your heart is His.

You, LORD, are the God our ancestors worshiped,
and from heaven you rule every nation in the world.
You are so powerful that no one can defeat you.
—2 Chronicles 20:6

Good King Jehoshaphat got some bad news:
Some messengers came to tell him that a great
multitude was on the march toward Judah to do
battle. So the king gathered the people together
to ask for God's help, and he prayed this prayer.

Then they stood and waited for God's response. God spoke through a prophet in response: "Your Majesty and everyone from Judah
and Jerusalem, the LORD says that you don't need
to be afraid or let this powerful army discourage
you. God will fight on your side!" (v. 15).

God knows. He hears. He answers. Jehoshaphat boldly approached Him and called
Him to answer according to His wisdom and
power. And He did.

And He will for you, too. Ask Him. Then wait
for His response.

Then he explained his plan and appointed men to march in front of the army and praise the LORD for his holy power by singing: "Praise the LORD! His love never ends."

—*2 Chronicles 20:21*

Jehoshaphat encouraged his people as they faced a major battle. Early in the morning, he went to the people gathered in the wilderness of Tekoa and said, "Listen my friends, if we trust the LORD God and believe what these prophets have told us, the LORD will help us, and we will be successful" (v. 20).

It all came down to faith. If they would trust God, He would be with them. If not, they would be on their own as they faced the enemy.

You may be facing a battle today. A tough day at work, a difficult conflict in a relationship, an important step forward in your personal growth. Remember God. Trust Him. And before you march out, sing His praises and contemplate His character.

Why are you disobeying me and my laws? This will
only bring punishment! You have deserted me, so
now I will desert you.

—2 Chronicles 24:20

Under Joash the nation unraveled again. The
people abandoned God, forsook His temple, ignored His word.

The word of the Lord came on Zechariah,
who stood before the people and asked them the
question in today's reading: Why do you break
the Lord's laws? Their sin obviously had a negative impact on their lives, yet they were blind to
it. But because they had deserted God, He had
deserted them.

It's a sad story. And it has been repeated often
in the Old Testament record.

But the story continues today. You know of individuals who stubbornly refuse to turn to God;
they keep fighting Him and struggling against
Him in an effort to gain a personal victory—
which in reality is nothing but defeat.

Look at yourself. Are you truly following God,
pursuing His will, yearning for His presence in
your life?

DAY 358

But the children of those officers were not killed; the LORD had commanded in the Law of Moses that only the people who sinned were to be punished.

—*2 Chronicles 25:4*

One incident early in Amaziah's reign showed his obedience to the "Law of Moses." He had the servants executed who had murdered his father, the king. But he did not put their children to death because of the Lord's command noted in today's reading (from Deut. 24:16).

God is a just God. He must punish sin. But that punishment has a boundary: Each individual is responsible only for his or her life. If children sin, parents will not be put to death. If parents sin, children will be spared.

The truth is, we all sin. We are responsible for our own behavior. God has provided a way out of that death sentence: He sent His own Son, Jesus Christ, to take upon Himself the punishment for all the sin of humankind.

In the first month of the first year of Hezekiah's rule, he unlocked the doors to the LORD's temple and had them repaired.

—2 Chronicles 29:3

Hezekiah assumed the reins of leadership in Judah, and he did what was right in God's eyes. One of his very first acts was to open the doors of the temple and repair them. That practical, yet symbolic, act was necessary because of Ahaz's idolatry.

Ahaz had closed up the temple, locked its doors, and cut up all the articles of worship. And he had set up altars for himself on every corner in Jerusalem. It was idolatry run rampant.

Hezekiah repaired the doors and opened them up to the people. This is the way to God, his actions declared. This is the only way. For He is the only God.

Throughout life, we must close some doors and open new ones. What doors have you closed that need to be repaired and opened today?

The enemies that have captured your families will show pity and send them back home. The LORD God is kind and merciful, and if you turn back to him, he will no longer turn his back on you.

—2 Chronicles 30:9

Hezekiah sent messengers to summon the people of Israel to return to Jerusalem for the sacred celebration of Passover. It had been a long time.

Regardless of what happened, the nation's sin was so deep that the people would indeed face captivity in a foreign land. But if they humbled themselves and returned to the Lord, God would treat their children with compassion during that time, and they would ultimately return to the land.

God is faithful to keep after the wandering heart. He keeps giving opportunities to return to the fold. But it takes great courage to hear Him and come to Him in humility. Are you ignoring a summons of God in your life?

DAY 361

LORD God, these people are unclean according to the laws of holiness. But they are worshiping you, just as their ancestors did. So, please be kind and forgive them.

—2 Chronicles 30:18–19

It had been a long time since the people had gathered to celebrate Passover. And they were woefully out of practice. In fact, many of them had not ritually cleansed themselves in preparation for the event, due to ignorance or lack of time.

While most ignored the king's summons, a few came in obedience and humility back to the Lord in Jerusalem. They had come for cleansing and celebration. And King Hezekiah prayed that, despite their uncleanness, God would nevertheless provide atonement for them.

They had not prepared themselves physically for the event, but they had prepared their hearts to seek the Lord. And that was what was important.

God looks on the heart. His ways are established to enable us to come to Him clean and free. But He will always respond to a tender, open heart. No matter where you are, no matter the condition of your life, if your heart is right, God is ready to accept you in His presence.

DECEMBER 26

Ever since the people have been bringing us their offerings, we have had more than enough food and supplies. The LORD has certainly blessed his people. Look at how much is left over!

—*2 Chronicles 31:10*

Hezekiah's example of selfless giving to the temple had a major effect on his people. He commanded them to contribute to the priests and Levites, and they responded because they knew he was following his own command.

As a result, the children of Israel gave in abundance. After three months of generous giving, the offerings lay in heaps. And the heaps kept growing for several more months.

For one brief glimpse, we see what can happen when people's hearts are lubricated with generosity. They still have enough and more. They are able to give generously, and the giving opens the way for more abundance—physical and spiritual—from God's hand.

When we can humble ourselves and open our hands, God can go to work. Try it.

I am King Cyrus of Persia. The LORD God of heaven, who is also the God of Israel, has made me the ruler of all nations on earth. And he has chosen me to build a temple for him in Jerusalem, which is in Judah.

—Ezra 1:2–3

The tribes of Israel had long been scattered, sent fleeing from their land at the hand of their enemies. And though Judah had lasted longer, that nation, too, had been taken captive to Babylon. But God's promise prevailed. And He stirred up the heart of King Cyrus to issue a command for God's people to return to Jerusalem and rebuild the temple of God.

Can you imagine the incredible joy the people must have felt? Can you also imagine the fear of the unknown that lay before them? Still, their hearts were stirred. They knew God's promise, and they realized He was keeping it. And nothing was more important than being part of that.

Do you sense that God is at work, and that He wants you to be part of something great? Let Him stir your heart, too.

Let the Jewish governor and leaders rebuild it where it stood before. And stop slowing them down!

—Ezra 6:7

The locals were not happy. The Israelites had long been gone, and their land had come under the authority of others. But they were returning and rebuilding their city. Tattenai, the governor of the region, sent a letter to King Darius complaining about the situation.

A search was made of the records, and Cyrus's order was clear. Therefore, Darius sent word to Tattenai: The Jews were to rebuild their temple in their land.

It's nice to have friends in high places. The word of the king can silence the strongest critic. You may not have that luxury, however, at least in earthly terms.

But you have a Friend in the highest place possible: God Himself. He will always act on your behalf when you are engaged in His work. In the face of opposition, you can always call on Him for help and support. He will hear and answer.

The people started crying when God's Law was read to them. Then Nehemiah the governor, Ezra the priest and teacher, and the Levites who had been teaching the people all said, "This is a special day for the LORD your God. So don't be sad and don't cry!"

—Nehemiah 8:9

Nehemiah took upon himself the responsibility to rebuild the city walls of Jerusalem. He returned from Babylon to lead the massive undertaking. Ultimately, the wall was rebuilt.

To Nehemiah, the Word of God was so vital to life that he called the people together and had Ezra the scribe read the Scriptures to them for three hours each day. They listened. They heard. They responded. They worshiped. And they wept mournfully for how far their nation had fallen. But it was a holy day. Mourning was no longer necessary. It was a time of joy and hope, a time for God's promise to be fulfilled.

What are you mourning today? Is it time to put that behind you and look ahead once again?

DAY 366

Remember me, O my God, for good!
—*Nehemiah 13:31 (NKJV)*

Nehemiah's last words formed a simple prayer, using a theme that he had woven throughout his book: He prayed for God's blessing.

"Remember me." It's a prayer that is continually on our hearts. We fear abandonment. We dread rejection. And when we experience these things at the hands of important people in our lives—our parents, friends, mates—they create deep wounds that we must work hard to heal.

And because of these painful experiences, we may assume God will treat us the same way. We want to be significant to Him. We want our lives to make a difference. We want to be blessed.

But we can be confident that this is a prayer God will always hear and answer. We are never out of His thoughts, never separated from His plan. He actively seeks our good, sovereignly moves us through our lives, and graciously blesses us with His mercy and love. Draw strength from that truth.

DECEMBER 31

SUBJECT INDEX